THE PROM KING

BOUGHT A FRANCHISE

CHARACTERS FROM HIGH SCHOOL
FOLLOWED YOU INTO FRANCHISING

BY BOB GRIFFIN

Dedication

This is the last part of the book I worked on and the toughest to write. Authoring a book on franchising is not high on the list when you are asked what you want to do for a living. I started and restarted this book far more than I care to think about. Along the way, there are a few souls who asked me to keep going. This is me thanking you for never giving up on me.

Rachel has been my best friend and wife for more than two decades. I could not have worked in franchising without her support. Rachel is an amazing person, and I am thankful to have her in my life. I am not just saying that because she has all my money. Rachel, you are the love of my life.

James is my son and my BudBud. I tell him all the time that I was born to be his dad. He is the reason I want to work hard at being a successful man. Knowing the work I do is "watched like a hawk" by James makes me always want to do the right thing. I love you, son.

Thank you to Courtney Mosley for agreeing to do the drawings for the book. You are a wonderful artist in every sense of that word. You show us the wonder in the faces and places we see every day. Your talent was there when we first met, and you drew a picture of me as an elf. I love your work and am grateful to have you as part of my book. Thank you, my friend!

Thank you to all of the friends I have made in the years I have worked in the world of franchising. There are too many of you to mention. You pushed me to find ways to help you grow and, in that struggle, I learned a lot about business and life. I am grateful for the journey.

Finally, I want to thank my parents, Allen and Joan Griffin. My Dad always talked about writing the "Great American Novel". I do not think that is what this book is, Dad. However, I am glad that you planted the thought of authoring a book in my head. You have given me great advice and ideas all my life. That is what good dads do.

My Mama is an English teacher. Whatever bad grammar you find in here is not because she did not try her darnedest to teach me. I did not always listen. Watching her selflessly raise six kids showed me how to be a servant leader even before that term was coined. Thank you for being my Mama and God bless all teachers.

Introduction

Franchising is like being in high school. As much as we in the industry talk about franchising as being a "family" or a "culture" or some other comforting thing in your life, it is honestly like being back in high school. The reason no one talks about franchising being like high school is that we spent all our time in high school trying to get out. That would not make a good sales pitch.

High school and franchising are more alike than anyone is comfortable talking about. There is a system that you must follow, people you must deal with and none of it makes too much sense. Your entire knowledge base comes from the fact that you are required to follow along, or you will be kicked out.

High school was a time when all that you thought you knew about getting ahead in life was tested. You figured out a system for surviving your days there and had all sorts of strange people trying to mess things up for you. That sounds like franchising, doesn't it? High school was where you learned about friends, foes, and fears. Life in high school made you who you are now. You are an older, wiser, more neurotic version of that kid, and now you are looking to make it rich in franchising. While you read, pick out the friends, foes, and fears that will can hold you back or help you succeed in franchising.

All that mess from high school was great training for the moment you decided to become a franchisee. There was a lesson learned every day whether you noticed you were learning it or not. You are a survivor! You went onto the battlefield that was high school and came out with a piece of paper that showed you survived and can make decisions in the real world.

Not once in this book will I call you sane. I will, however, always give you credit for being smarter. You learned to survive in high school. High school was bootcamp for dealing with the maniacal side of life. The simple fact that you managed that craziness and still made a passing grade shows that you can survive the craziness of a franchise and make a profit. It is the same thing, but with a different grading scale.

As a Franchise Consultant for the better part of twenty years, I have spent my days talking about franchising with people who are either in a franchise or want to be in a franchise. Most of the time when I speak with potential franchisees, they have already talked with some sales manager for a particular franchise and have a bunch of happy thoughts about what it will be like once they plunk down piles of cash for the opportunity to proudly display a brand name. Nowhere in the discussion are sales managers talking about all the crazy people they will be doing business within that happy brand. Make no mistake about it; it is not the brand that will test your guts and sanity. It is the people you are sharing the brand with that will make you question all those happy thoughts you had before you signed your Franchise Disclosure Document.

As for me, I am the guy with the calm voice and demeanor. My job is as a teacher. I guide you through the hallowed halls of franchising. Everyone wants to do something new while understanding what to expect. I manage your expectations. Like any good teacher, I am loved and hated. I am often forgotten when you leave your franchise brand since you do not need my help anymore. Sometimes, I am remembered fondly as the guy who let you know you can survive the tough situations that franchising throws at you. I'm there when you need help and give you all the credit when you build a great business. Being a teacher is a thankless job. Go hug a teacher. I will wait for you to come back.

How did I come to the realization that franchising is like high school? Years ago, I was talking with a gentleman (he seemed so nice and rational at the time) who wanted to buy a franchise license and was asking me a million questions when it occurred to me that he was acting like I did with my older brothers when I was ready to start high school. I was nervous about getting into something that looked familiar but with people I did not know. I was worried that I would not be liked or be accepted or, even worse, that I would be singled out as a problem and get the snot beat out of me. That guy was acting the same way. He had no idea what he was getting into and he wanted someone to tell him point-blank what he could expect. For good reason, he did not want to get the snot beaten out of him.

For me, likening franchising to high school is a nice way to let you know what to expect. High school was the first "great equalizer" in our lives. No one was going to get an easy ride and someone was going to get kicked out. Describing franchising like high school paints the picture that there are rewards as soon as you figure out how to make the system work for you. Nothing is easy, but there are rewards. It can be a good fit if you find the right path to follow and avoid the pitfalls of hanging out with the wrong crowd. Yes, your Momma was right. There is a wrong crowd, and they are a real pain in the backside in franchising. Find out who they are fast and keep a good distance.

If you want to win at anything, you need to know what level of harassment/stress/chaos you will deal with daily. In high school, that level was high. Maybe, that is why they call it high school. The stress is high, the work is at a much higher level than you had before, and the people you had to deal with were off the chart weirder than you ever thought you would meet.

Franchising is not easy. Feel free to verbally gut punch any sales weasel who tells you your new franchise "runs itself". It is not a cash machine that will spit out money just because you own it (unless you bought an ATM franchise). A franchise is a group of people and a business system that works (most of the time). Franchising is also a group of people with different ideas than you have, working together. The corporate office and the franchisees need to be a good mix or things break down. Do you remember any classes where the students did not work well together? Yes? Exchange "grades" for "thousands of dollars" and you can see why getting into the right place makes all the difference.

When you thought about leaving high school did you think you were finished with all those characters that made your life miserable? Or, as a matter of common sense, did you know they were graduating right beside you and that there are even more people like them from all of the other high schools around the country that you would soon have to deal with in life and business?

Common sense was not in the core curriculum in high school so you can be forgiven a little. I am sorry to burst your bubble of imagined sanity, but the same people you knew in high school are all around you every day. Since you bought into a franchise and are one of the freshmen franchisees, you are now doing business with those former high school classmates (*insert a full-body shiver here*). In fact, you are relying on the fact that they will do things the right way and not destroy your business by dragging down your reputation and your sales with their bad ideas. Now who is crazy, hmm?

High school was a time when every personality available had the opportunity to come out of hiding and stand right in front of you. Do you remember their pimply-faced smiles, "I forgot my homework" grimaces, or bad hairstyles? Back then, you had to deal with those characters in class and do dangerous science experiments with them for a grade. Nothing changes your way of thinking like the possibility of an explosion for a grade. Those same kids that creeped you out are all grown up now, and they are still way too close to you. On top of that, they are still doing things that you should probably wear safety goggles to be nearby. Life and business ownership are all about how you get what you need from people you do not want to hang out with at any time of the day.

The sales guy is going to talk about the franchisees being "family" because he will not get your money if he tells you the franchisees act like they are counting the days until spring break. What type of person would willingly join something that made him think of his high school years? Some of us are far past high school and are nostalgic for those years. Go look at the kids coming out of any high school. Are they disappointed that the school day ended? Of course not! Now stop being sentimental and get back to reality. The sales guy is playing a shell game to keep you on the hook. He does not want to be your beloved franchise uncle. He wants your money.

This book is my view at franchising from the perspective of decades as an Operations Management Analyst/Consultant and Corporate Trainer. I have written franchise manuals, store opening guides, and trained hundreds of people on how to be successful. I have been the "designated thug" to have to tell franchisees any and all bad news, including taking away their franchise. I have been shot-at and stabbed in my line of work. Despite that, I will tell you that there is no better way to get into business than in a good franchise system. I love franchising. Anyone who is in franchising for more than ten years will tell you how great it is. It may just be that we get slightly warped by the experience of going to a job that has all the same weird people we ran from once we received a diploma, but we love it all the same. Franchising works...most of the time.

Enjoy the book and start picking out the people in your franchise (or in your life outside of the franchise) that I describe here. I added ways to deal with them since that is the way to be successful in franchising. Each chapter has a description of a personality type you probably dealt with in high school. There are personal stories to give perspective. Some of the chapters have homework and some of them have a field trip or bonus questions to help your grade. The book was written to be a quick read and get you thinking about how you dealt with the people you are surrounded with in life. The more you know how others think, the easier it is to get what you need from or with them. Quit being pushed around like a freshman and start thinking strategically like a senior. Find a good place to study and do your homework neatly. Penmanship is important.

Your real job in a franchise is figuring out how to make things work for you.

Cheers!

Bob Griffin
Business Bulldog Brands
Chief Bulldog-in-Charge

The Syllabus

1. Welcome Freshmen!
2. Your Classmates Think You're A Dork
3. The Class Clown Even Smells Funny
4. The Brainiac Still Can't Figure It Out
5. The Nerd Is Dark and Mysterious
6. The Jock – Beer, Boobies, and Balls
7. The Cheerleader Was Exhausting
8. The Kid Everyone Knew But No One Knew Anything About
9. That Damn Bully
10. Teachers Are People Too
11. Guidance Counselors Don't Use GPS
12. The Principal Had Better Things to Do
13. Cliques – You're Not as Cool as You Remember
14. Ugh! Homework!
15. There Are Grades? What the…
16. Another Year of This?? REALLY!?!
17. The Prom King Can't Dance
18. There Is No Summer Break In Franchising
19. There's A Whole New Freshman Class Coming In
20. The Senior Class Project
21. Graduate! You sell out

Lesson 1

Welcome Freshmen!

Welcome freshmen franchisees! Things are going to be interesting as you start your adventure of learning in these poorly painted classrooms. There will be pop quizzes and field trips for you to get some extra credit. You didn't sail through high school, and you aren't going to sail through your time as a franchisee. Nothing worth working for is easy.

Your franchise freshman year is designed to push you. There will be times when you are the happiest you have ever been, and there will be emotional breakdowns. If these walls could talk, they'd tell you that you weren't the first one to take this path, and you won't be the last.

The freshman year in anything is designed to kick your butt. No offense but being nice to you during your freshman year in high school would have made you into more of a whimpering mess than you already were. Stress keeps you sharp, and we all want to be sharp when we are working toward a goal. Your freshman year in a franchise is exactly the same. Everything looks similar and easy, but actually getting the hang of things is going to take time and requires that you change everything you think you understand. Your fellow freshmen will be friends until they find ways to get ahead of you. Everyone will be making mental notes on how you work and what you look like doing it. Freshman year is like volunteering to be a punching bag. Good luck!

The benefit of being in franchising over being in high school is that following the rules gets you more stuff. In this case, the more stuff you get is money. A good grade in calculus is not going to move the needle, but earning profits opens doors. Smart freshmen in franchising get that concept and work to make it happen quickly.

How do you make things work when, instead of grades, you are looking to turn a profit? Dealing with people is the best part of what you already learned in high school. Those are lessons from high school that should never be forgotten. You survived and graduated! That is success. Congratulations! High-fives for everyone!

There are students in franchising who think they can out-maneuver everyone and get ahead. They think they can be the "Big Boss" and hand the reigns to an employee to run the business. Freshmen have interesting ways of thinking about everything. The panic of having to face years of going back to the same place and being judged on your work is daunting.

High school showed you how to make things work with the geeks, the jocks, and the cheerleaders. The best business owners understand this and wake up each day relying on those learned skills and the right attitude to deal with it.

Every business is a people business. How you relate to the people that you partner with under a brand name determines how long you are in your franchise and how profitable you will be. It is not a math problem, but it kind of sounds like one. It is a people problem, and we are going to walk through the basics of people solving to make the grade.

Just so we get these ideas straight, poor people-skills are one of the top reasons that people fail. Franchisees do not take into account all of the personalities that they encounter daily when they are trying to sell products and services or deal with other people in business. Starting with the employees they hire and going all the way to the vendors they owe for products, freshmen business owners can either take the time to build a relationship with every part of their franchise or they can fight a losing battle when things get tough.

Note #1

Here is a hint on making it all work: Start your time as a franchisee knowing that you need to learn not only about the system for making money but also the people who make it work. That will help give you a back-up plan when things get rough. Most people will help a friend if asked. Creating a friendship starts before there is a need for a friend. Do you remember that lesson from high school? Do you remember that weird kid who ate lunch alone? That kid never got any help. Now, he is two miles down the road from you as a franchisee in the same brand and weirder than ever. That little hint I mentioned at the beginning of this paragraph was also part of every grade in high school. Now, thank your Momma for telling you to go make friends.

But wait! The problem in franchising is that the people you remember from high school, the crazy ones, are now in business with you. You spent most of your time in your teen years trying to avoid these people. Now, am I really asking you to become friends with them? Yes. The fun of how to make that happen is in the next few chapters.

Crazy is an art form. I like that saying. I may have to put that saying on a T-shirt.

When you started high school, you thought you were normal and level-headed and had the makings of greatness. You thought it was only a matter of time before you were the most popular person in the school and got all A's because, well, you were you. I hate to be the bearer of bad news, but you were crazy too. The art of being crazy is that every one of your fellow students thought the same way you did, and they also thought YOU were nuts. Bless your stupid high school heart. It is tough to know that you were crazier than a room full of bats when you started high school because you only saw things from your own perspective. Hindsight is ugly.

The kids who knew how crazy things looked were also the ones who knew how to make the system work. You saw those kids slide around school without a hitch. They knew everyone and everyone knew them. They were invited to parties that you wished you could have gone to and they had friends around every corner.

That kid was not the most popular because being the center of attention limited his access to everything. He was not the prom king either. He was just clever and knew the rules to follow. That is the kid I want you to be now that you have a mortgage and kids to drop off at scout meetings. You are still one of the crazy ones. Look in the mirror and honestly tell me I am wrong. The best part is that now that you have a few years under your belt; you know there is a better way to make everything work.

Age is a beautiful thing. It gives you perspective and the courage to look at things differently. It also slows you down, and you do not have the energy to be a "badass". Let's call that "God's Little Joke".

Following a system that you pay a lot of good money to get into is the simple part. Dealing with the less pimply faced but still nutty people you remember from high school is where the money is made. Get ready to be a kid again. OK, maybe a better version of who you were when the squeal of the school bus brakes made you cringe.

Field Trip

It is time to go visit all of the businesses in your area that are doing what you want to do. Take a notebook and a smile. You are going to take a really good look at the people working in the businesses. Can you work with any of them? What if they came in with a bad attitude? What would you do? Write an essay on what type of employee you want to hire and why.

Homework #1:

1. What are the best elements of what you saw on your field trip?
2. What does the perfect employee look like, sound like, and act like?
3. Can you train hourly employees who will only put up with so much stress before they quit and walk down the street for another hourly job?
4. What senses, besides eyesight, did you use when you were at the locations? What stands out the most?
5. How did you feel when you were in the location? Was there a business that had a better "feel"?
6. What would you add to your business that you liked from what you saw in the other businesses?
7. What questions would you ask an applicant to be able to find the best employees you saw in the businesses?
8. What makes a great business?
9. How often did you see or interact with the manager? Was he/she available if you asked to speak with him/her?
10. Did the real estate make a difference in the way the customers came into the business? What does that tell you about where you should locate your business?

Lesson 2

Your Classmates Think You're a Dork

There is no better place to start than with you. You were nowhere near as cool as you thought. You still are not. You were/are a dork. Take it easy. Everyone was/is a dork. If you do not believe me, look at your old high school yearbook. It is a walk down a dark lane of memories with a big spotlight on bad hair styles. Dorky is just one way to live your life. Dorky is avoidable, though. You just need to think of things in terms of nothing being permanent. It will not work, but you can think about anything. Try it.

Get a good look in those yearbook pages and the people you remember from high school. Now, look at the people in your franchise brand. Those are the same people who make your life insane now as you try to tackle being an owner in a franchise that you want to work to provide a better living for you and your family. And, yes, your high school classmates did think you were a dork. It took the attention away from how dorky they were when they were rocking Swatch watches and neon-colored pants. I grew up in the eighties. Can you tell?

If you want to avoid being the dork, you need to plan for things to last way past the immediate future. Legacy brands think this way. They plan for decades and centuries, not for what can make them trendy for the moment. Trendy businesses like that thankfully die out quickly. Plan for what you want your business to look like when you are retired and look back at what you created. No one will call you a dork for planning for a strong future. OK, so someone will call you a dork, just not anyone worth listening to. Do not worry about the naysayers. They will be coming by for a job later when their businesses go under. Now I see you smiling!

There is a story in those pictures in your yearbook. Can you read the story in the pictures? There are personalities that came rushing out once everyone made it to high school. As for learning who those people were, the first thing we learned about them allowed us to dump them into mental buckets. We kept them there all through high school since it was easier to work with what we thought. We knew who we were dealing with when we had to deal with them.

Mostly, our first impressions of people came by what the students wore to school. If they were trendy, we dumped them into a bucket. If they were geeky, they got their own bucket. Jocks smelled like jocks. They got their own bucket with an air freshener. You can see the trend here. You did that for every student you went to school with. That does not make you a bad person. It makes you lazy. Not a bad person, though.

Feel free to have another full body shiver when you think about your own high school "choices". Calling you dorky is being kind. None of the "cool" things you did in high school were actually cool. Cool was reserved for that kid who knew everyone was dorky and he was OK with that fact. He was the kid that walked to his own beat and let everyone know he was going to be his own man. He was nice to everyone since he figured that everyone was walking to some weird drumbeat that only he could hear. You were nervous about being seen and he was seen everywhere. Can you think of a time when you were really comfortable at school? Yeah, me neither. But that is the difference. Now that you are older and too tired to give a damn, be comfortable and rock to your own beat.

Note #2

So, why did one kid make high school and everything in life look so easy?

This was a guy who met everyone at his or her own level and made friends. I cannot emphasize enough how important it is to see people for who they are and how they see themselves. It does not matter if you agree with their way of thinking or acting. All that matters is that they do not get in your way of making money and building your own business.

You are in a franchise where you have lots of people who need your attention, and you want to be seen as anything but dorky. So, be cool. Make friends. No, you do not need to go on vacation with them. That's plain weird. You only need to be good with who *they are* and deal with their quirks. They are not going to change. Are you going to change your personality? Of course you aren't. Do not expect them to change. Deal with your own hang ups and enjoy dealing with your fellow franchisees and their hang ups.

So, how do you make friends with these crazy kids when you really want to lock the door when you see them coming? Ah, the fun of being in a franchise is that it is all a system to follow. Even dealing with dorky, crazy people is a system. The trick is to meet them at their level of nuttiness. That, my friends, is the system that I live in every day. I have a great job.

Every person has a "set of buttons" that make him or her really angry, sad, happy, or intently listen. Find the right button and press it when you need the other person to act in a certain way and you will get everything you need from your franchise. There really is not a button. Do not go touching people. That invites problems I am not going to talk about in this book.

Let us start by breaking the franchisees into the groups you saw in high school. The class clown, the jock, and the cheerleader were in every high school. If you can see those people the way they see themselves, you can work within a set of guidelines that leads them through life. High school formed their self image. It is time to start using that to build your business.

Over the next few chapters, we will learn all about the personalities that once entertained you through your teen years. Time to have some fun!

Homework#2:

1. Do you know what you act like when you are tired? Stressed?
2. What is the worst personality that you can still talk with without punching him in the throat?
3. If someone wants to push your buttons and make you angry, how hard does he need to push? Can you control it?
4. What type of person would make you lock the door and not serve?
5. What type of person would you never hire? Is it a look, a personality, or something else?
6. What would you do if your worst enemy from high school bought the store down the street from you?
7. Is there a time, now that you are an adult, that you are most relaxed and do not care what happens around you? Yes, you still have to be mentally functional.
8. Was there a time in high school when you got along with very different people from whom you thought you were?

Lesson 3

The Class Clown Even Smells Funny

Every high school has a loveable troublemaker. When I remember those "cut ups" I cringe and I smile at the same time. There are class clowns in any group of people. Class clowns are the kids who are smart kids who get bored. They knew just when to get into trouble and wanted the teacher's and everyone else's attention often. Maybe they were lonely or just wanted to be recognized. They were peers that everyone in the class, at one time or another, had to deal with directly. It was never a good thing to deal with him directly, but you had to. He was usually picking on you for being a wimp or making fun of your off-brand sneakers. He was not really a bully. He was just going for laughs. Of course, it did not feel like he was just going for a laugh back in high school. He was a true pain in your seated parts.

He (it seemed to always be a guy - right ladies?) created pranks to get the class laughing. One day in my high school the class clown released a garter snake in class. That was both a fun morning and also a time when I thought my teacher was going to die at school. Teachers do not like snakes. OK, so a lot of students do not like a slithering snake sliding around a classroom either. When the class clown started laughing before the snake was released, we kinda knew who did it. He was marched down to the principal's office, and we didn't see him for a few days. He came back to the class as a legend and a lot more cautious than we remembered him being. That incident made me think that the class clown can be worked with on a different level.

Dealing with someone who needs a lot of attention and wants to have fun can be a laugh-riot in the short run and disastrous if you get stuck doing business near his store. Remember how serious you thought certain things were in high school? There were a lot of serious people in high school. It was because no one wanted to be seen as a dork. You still live your life in the pursuit of not looking stupid. How much time did you take to get ready for work today? See?? Sometime around high school, wearing the right clothes and trying to be popular made you into a squeaky clean serious person. The class clown saw you coming before you even left your house.

How did you deal with a class clown in high school? Did you give him lots of room and laugh when he made a joke? Or, as you do now, did you scold him and tell the teacher? You gave him the room he needed when you were younger and going with your gut. He is, after all, funny and in need of some attention. What makes you think he has changed since high school? You can hope that his wife and kids give him the attention he needs, but more than likely, they are just like him.

The kid in you wants to join him in a few drinks and a few pranks. You want to have the fun you neglected to have in high school. That is something you should save for when you are in Vegas or somewhere far from people who know you or where there are few cameras to record your wild ways.

Success in dealing with a fellow franchisee who is a time and energy hog and, even worse, a detriment to your building a solid customer base requires that you look at things from his perspective. Yes, you have to look at business through a clown's eyes.

The class clown franchisee got into business because he wanted to be his own boss. He did not like anyone telling him what to do. He is also a smart guy and knows he does not want to take the time to do a marketing plan or create a business from the ground up. That is what franchising does best. A class clown franchisee is not going to be the best franchisee or help you build the brand. He is in this for the chance to not have a boss that would tell him what to do or grade him on his operations. There, my friend is where you have an opening into making him behave like he just got caught with another snake to release.

Franchising is a system that you are legally required to follow once you sign the documents. It is a contract. The space for doing things your own way or creating problems is a thin area at best and does not exist at all in great franchises. Everyone who buys into a franchise needs to follow the steps required to operate his business the same way or he will get a warning, a restriction, or get kicked out. That sounds like high school, doesn't it?

Class clown franchisees are trouble but can be made to behave reasonably well. Class clown franchisees want attention. Getting caught being bad is attention and so is getting caught doing the right thing. Once you remind him that he can cut up with the customers or, even better, go somewhere else to have fun since he can hire a manager to run things, he sees a clear picture. He is the boss and he needs to find the space to be serious about his business. They do not need to ruin their business to be the center of attention. He will get more attention from everyone in the franchise when he starts doing things the right way. Your job, to save yourself from his clowning, is to find the times when they are doing something right like hiring a good employee or when you hear good customer feedback.

Now do you see where I am going? Telling others when the class clown franchisee is doing the right thing helps you and him. He behaves and you keep him from pulling a prank on you. Remember that you are the same brand to customers. Spend time and resources on building your business even if it is building his at the same time.

On the franchisor side of the fence, getting a testimonial statement from someone who was doing things the wrong way because they wanted to "show us how to have fun in business" and is now following the system is the attention the brand and a class clown needs. Trying to get buy-in from many different people in a franchise is tough. Helping the franchisor control a class clown with positive reinforcement is a huge way to improve your standing in the franchise.

Class clowns like having an audience, so give them one when they act the way you need them to. Also, watch out for times when they are acting like something is about to happen. Class clowns suck at being sneaky. Getting caught was all part of the act for them.

Note #3

Class clowns are rare as adults. We lose our sense of humor. We laugh less as we age. We smile less as adults. They end up being the ones you see are in an office asking everyone before noon if they want to go to lunch. They are not that popular anymore. No one wants to hang out with a guy who will fill the office with crickets for a laugh.

There is value in finding and working with a class clown adult. As adults, they are creative thinkers. As a franchisee, if you do have a class clown franchisee near you, you can use him to find creative ways to crush the competition. Your competition is thinking of devious ways to torpedo your business. Why not invite a guy who has made a life out of messing with people into developing a plan with you to mess with the competitors.

There are ground rules. There is no need to spend too much time with him. Make sure you set meeting times and an agenda. Do not invite him to your store. He will start looking for ways to mess with you. Also, make sure you have a defined end to playtime. If you do not, he will keep coming back to one-up his games.

Homework #3:

Dealing with class clowns is all about giving them the right attention. Get a guy like me involved and give them a new direction to go.

1. Do not try to fight with a class clown. It does not work. What button do you think gets pushed to make him pick on someone?
2. Do not try to prank him back when he makes you the butt of the joke. He will look to "one-up" you...and will. How much attention will you get for the wrong reason?
3. Do not try to work through the problems a class clown franchisee creates alone. At what point can you handle a class clown and when should you call the franchisor representative for help?
4. When a class clown franchisee starts to behave well give him attention. Redirecting his energy is the best way to reinforce what you need him to do. What is a good way to provide the class clown with the right kind of attention?
5. Do not start mentioning his old ways. It will just get him thinking about causing trouble again. What are safe subjects to talk about with a class clown?
6. When there is another franchisee who is causing you grief, point the class clown toward him. OK, that isn't good advice, but it can be fun. Can you get away with pointing to a class clown at a problem?

Lesson 4

The Brainiac Still Can't Figure It Out

The brainiac was the opposite of the class clown. He or she was smart, of course, and had to know the answer to everything. He was the first to raise his hand when the teacher asked for an answer. Truth be told, he was the only one to raise his hand. He was our savior in school since we did not study as much as we should have (and still do not). He was a dork, but he was also the kid that you turned to when you were stuck on a math problem or forgot your notes at school and there was a test the next day.

He was lonely just like the class clown, but he did not want to be seen as a troublemaker. Of course, he was lonely because no one knew what the hell he was talking about. Watching British television shows and thinking jocks are stupid was comforting to him. If he could go to a class where there were no other students and the teacher asked lots of questions that he had answers to, he would be happy. For all his intelligence, he did not work on his social skills and went to the prom alone or with other smart kids.

Smart kids were/are seen as "different" in high school. They were going to get into college and have a great life. We were all sure of that. I mean, how could life be bad when they could think their way through any problem? But, there was a problem they couldn't think their way out of and that is where they get stuck as a franchisee. If no one can relate to you then no one can get to know you. Brainiacs live lonely lives, very different from class clowns. They can talk for hours on any topic and not notice that everyone left the room. For that reason, they are not good franchisees.

As for hiring staff, if you cannot relate to anyone, why would anyone want to work for you? There are a few rules that all businesses live by to be successful. I call them the Bulldog Rules for Business. You can find them at my website BusinessBulldog.com. One of them, Bulldog Rule #14 says, "The right people never want to work with the wrong people." Does it seem too simple a rule? I can tell you stories of how great a rule it is and how many businesses fail because of not following that one rule. I will save those stories for another book.

If you are a brainiac franchisee, you need to find someone who is almost as smart as you (I say that because you are never going to believe anyone could be as smart as you are). Make this "almost as smart as you" person your business manager and get out of the way. Visit your manager when you need to know how the business is running and whether the budget is being followed. Other than that, you need to leave everything alone.

Brainiac franchisees are a pain to talk with and understand. Since many franchises are run by hourly employees and they need quick instructions to do their job, a brainiac franchisee is not going to be able to find employees without help.

Be smart and give your business the room to hire great employees who are not going to be intimidated by you. Smart is an action word. I tell my son that smart is not what you know. Smart is what you do. Do smart things.

Would a brainiac get the meaning of "Do smart things"? No, he would not. He thinks he is smarter than me.

Sometimes all of us are the wrong people for the job. Even if you invented the job you are in, there will be times when you need to pass along the responsibility to someone else to get you to the next level. Business owners usually get this lesson wrong. Either they jump out of the way too quickly and leave the person in charge with no directions or they do not leave fast enough, and they get in the way of any growth that could happen. You'd think that a guy who can out-think everyone would be able to see this and make it work but, he is the one who loses everything a few times over until he finds someone he trusts to hand the keys to the business to operate it for him.

Note #4

A brainiac is the toughest person to work with in franchising. Finding a way to talk with a brainiac is tough. He is the guy who thinks he already knows everything and then you are going to ask him to listen to you as you try to help both of you succeed in a franchise. Sounds like a great "Buddy Movie".

Start by asking lots and lots of questions. Look amazed at the depth of his knowledge and be ready to ask follow-up questions that you think he can answer. Stumping him with a question he cannot answer only makes him feel stupid. A brainiac who cannot answer a question makes him run for cover. This is not a good thing when you are looking for him to help you grow sales.

Walk him to a corner with questions so that he feels he has to show you how smart he is and will do what you want him to do. For example, ask questions about what customers want and how much they will pay. Once he is fully entrenched in talking about how easy it is to manipulate people, ask him to show you. Mention that you had an idea for a sale, but were not sure how to make it work.

Homework #4:

1. How would you make the brainiac franchisee think all ideas came from him? Yeah, you thought up the idea, but without him thinking it through, it wouldn't have worked. You get the money, and he can have the credit.
2. What would you do if you disagree with a brainiac? He does not understand that he is offensive when he has to be right all the time.
3. When would be a good time to spend time listening to him? All you have to do is nod your head and smile when you get lost in his explanations. Some of what he says will make sense. He is trying to communicate.
4. He is essentially harmless…until he thinks he can run his store better than the franchise can and makes his own changes. Does your franchise post customer feedback for all the franchisees to see? Can you request to see everyone's feedback?
5. When would you bring your operations guy in to get involved? The operations guy is a good buffer and keeper of the peace between the two of you.
6. How can you weave the Franchise Agreement into a conversation with a brainiac? Talking about the Franchise Agreement as a reference guide with him makes him have to know everything about it. He will weirdly cite it from memory and realize he needs to follow it. He is not original or creative.

He will push you to follow it too. And that's a good thing.

7. How can you make him like you? If he thinks you like him, he will give you some room to work with him on local marketing plans. Getting collaboration going on local store marketing with a brainiac makes things run profitably. They look at the process like you read a book. That level of detail in ROI (return on investment) is crucial when targeting customers.

8. You are smart as well or you would not be a franchisee along with him. When do you stand up to his smart jabbering so you can get to the point? He never had friends in high school. He may be making up time for that.

Bonus Points

Brainiacs are often obsessive compulsive. If he ticks you off to the point of no return, find out what bothers him most and mess it up. I had one brainiac franchisee obsess about clean windows. The other franchisees he was bothering came by every night just to rub a bar of soap over his front window. It was stupid, but funny.

Teacher's note:

A great man I happen to be related to told me that everyone is smart in his own way. It took me most of my life to realize that truth. Brainiacs are limited by their own intelligence. Trying to change someone is stupid. Embrace who they are and what they can do to help you accomplish in your franchise.

Leave the rest alone.

Lesson 5

The Nerd Is Dark and Mysterious

The nerd is not the same as the brainiac. I put these two identities beside each other so you could see the differences. The nerd is the kid that is just off center. He knows it and likes it that way. Nerds are often smart and have some things that they do well. They like to work alone or in small groups of nerds and have a way of looking at things that are outside of normal or average.

I do not want nerds anywhere to think I am calling them dangerous by the title of this chapter. Nerds are not dangerous. Nerdiness is a level of weirdness that gives new perspective to any situation. They are not interested in following social norms. They are not comfortable being around a lot of people. Trends form in groups of people, and they stand out since they think differently.

Nerds may have invented the social platforms that you use every day online, but they still cannot relate to anyone. Well, that is, unless it is a convention of other nerds who share the same level of odd outlook on everything. Want to see a new level of creativity? Go to one of those Sci-Fi conventions. It will make your convention look so boring!

That being said, a strange outlook can infect a franchise system and make a brand fail or, as I have seen first-hand, bring it to new heights. Every business wants to be known as unique. Being "weirdly unique" may not be a good thing. Trust in a brand is required in everything. Weird is not trustworthy. Weird is fun for a while. For nerdy individuals, looking at things your own way does not work well in a franchise (most of the time). A franchise works well when all franchisees follow a system. Add in dash of nerdy nuttiness to a franchise and you could have the makings of a spectacular failure that people will write about for centuries. They may even make action figures to commemorate it. OK, so that last sentence isn't going to deter a nerd from becoming a franchisee. It would be a brilliant disaster though.

I did mention that a nerd's weirdness could be a spectacular success. Marketing teams that are given the ability to be creative and are guided by the operations teams so that their ideas fit with what is already part of the system can show customers a new way of enjoying your products or services. Apps for ordering food have taken off, but it took someone looking at his phone and wanting to order a pizza. How crazy does that sound? But it works, and now we all spend at least a chunk of our days looking to our phones for service. Nerds can rule!

In high school, a nerd's nerdiness started when the class clown made a joke about him and everyone laughed. He never recovered from that and lives a secluded life to avoid that humiliation but comes out of his cave of solitude because he still wants to be seen. That does not sound like a good fit for franchising, does it?

I mentioned that nerd franchisees like to work alone or with others like them. Franchising requires that you work well with all kinds of people to make the system run. That's why this book works so well.

Unless your franchise is totally online, you are going to have problems working with a nerd franchisee. Not that a nerd wouldn't relish being your friend but he has had little practice being himself in public without people staring at him. He does not fit perfectly into the world. I think it makes him great and odd all at the same time. For you, as his neighbor in a franchise, it can make you a little off too.

Please do not make the mistake of thinking a nerd is stupid. These guys have all sorts of knowledge and survived high school just like you. He just did not show up for the graduation ceremony. No one noticed he was not there. Yep, it is sad. God bless his superhero-sized heart.

So, how does a nerd get into a franchise? There is a cascade of bad decisions that make it possible for someone who is more comfortable wearing a costume from a science fiction movie to operate in the same brand as you. Let us start that story back in high school.

In high school, this person was easy to see and given a wide berth. There was usually an unflattering nickname to identify him in case he was not around. The jocks cheated off his tests but also have him swirlies in the locker room. (Again, I am not going to go into what a swirlie is. Google is grand...swirlies, not so much.).

In a franchise, a sale can happen quickly and with little oversight. The sales dudes do not even need to meet a buyer. Just send them a check and see how fast they send you something to sign so they can get their commission. The franchise sales dude is usually only interested in getting a commission. I say usually because it is true. There are a few great sales guys who work hard to find a great match for the franchise. Those good guys do not usually survive in a franchise long. Deals turn wheels. If you are not wheeling and dealing, then you are not working. Anyway, dealing with a nerd franchisee after the check clears is the operations department's problem according to the sales duds (Yes, I spelled that right.).

A nerd is the kid who may want to fit in, but cannot find a foothold, so he wants to give up quickly without really trying. He is dark and mysterious because he lurks near the rest of society and lives vicariously through the characters he sees in films and TV. He wants to be that smart, fast, and strong hero. He thinks wanting those qualities is enough to get him everything in life. It is easier to lurk than to stand out. You have to be part of the group enough to be noticed for the good you bring before they will let you drive the business.

Sorry all my nerd friends. I cannot make you sound like an action figure when you cannot keep up with what everyone else your age is doing. If you want to be the leader, you have to leave your mom's basement.

Personally, I have a streak of nerdiness that will never leave me. I was teased in high school, and I still hold a part of me back from the world to keep from getting hit like that again. No, I do not own a costume or any Star Trek items. I have not gone to the Sci-Fi conventions either. Not that I have anything against them. They look like a lot of fun.

I do like the way nerds look at things to see something new. Nerds are creative. Creative people are worth the time and effort to get to know. Ask a nerd franchisee how to make a promotion better and he is going to bring everything to the table as soon as he trusts that you are not going to laugh at him. Want to explore new horizons in getting customers? Give carte blanche to a nerd franchisee. Want to know why Facebook, Twitter, and LinkedIn all work? The nerd who came up with it saw beyond what was already there. Now do you see?

For a nerd to be in a franchise though, it can be a daunting task for everyone involved. In a nerd franchisee's head, he sees himself as the guy from a movie that has the best life and a beautiful girlfriend. Real life is way, way different. Nerd franchisees are in business to be like those powerful people in comics and movies. They do not have a grasp on how to lead a team since no one ever listened to them in high school. Because they are loners, they often have horrible employees who run over them and do as they please. You have to have respect for yourself before anyone will respect you. I cannot teach respect as a consultant, but I can encourage the right aspects of leading employees. Respect comes after we show some success. For most of us, we think, "I can" and then go make it happen. For a nerd franchisee, he must say, "I can see it in my head" before he thinks, "I can do it."

A franchise run by a nerd franchisee is typically a mess since he ends up making his business look like he feels. He is not usually in business for long. Nerd franchisees still blame everyone for making them feel bad.

I do not like having to kick a nerd franchisee out of the franchise system. It feels wrong, but it is required sometimes. All stores in a franchise need to operate the same way. You cannot have a separate personality for each location. Customers will not get it and will go somewhere where they know what they are getting on each visit. Nerd franchisees can make a brand falter when they join.

Following a contract is not something a nerd does well either. It is too much like the popular kids telling them what to do. If a dark and mysterious nerd sets up shop near your store you can work with him on how to see their business as a safe place. When he is comfortable, he will listen and both of you can grow your businesses.

Note #5

Nerds think in ways you cannot or will not. You want to line things up and have them make sense. A nerd franchisee has the ability to ask, "What if..." and take it to an unheard-of way of looking at something. That freedom from constraints makes him valuable. Look for ways to use that thinking to increase sales.

What if you were to ask him, "What if" and finish the sentence with something that would bring in more customers? Such as, "What if we had an event to bring in people and have them donate to raise awareness of the plight of homeless children?" Watch what happens when a nerd franchisee see that he can help someone in need. There is a shift from being someone worried about being laughed at to being someone who can be a hero.

When you are going to start a conversation like this, be prepared for something over the top to be part of the discussion. Bring a budget and an outline. Let him fill in the blanks. Not only are you working with someone who is looking for a connection, but you are getting a new look at how an event can be created. He does not see things like you do. Enjoy the energy and creative mood.

This will be the entire conversation you will have until and after the event. Be prepared to be patient and thankful. He is willing to help you improve the brand image and help the community. Not enough people do this. Thankfulness is a great way to keep him on your team.

Homework #5:

1. How do you work with a nerd franchisee? Distance…lots of it…at first. How can you keep a distance and still work near a Nerd Franchisee?
2. If a nerd franchisee thinks he is dark and mysterious, he does not want to meet in an office. It is very un-mysterious to meet in an office on first contact. Do you think meeting him the first few times by email or Skype would work?
3. How would you communicate with a Nerd Franchisee? Use words like "mission" and "directive". Do not use his alter-ego name. Calling him "Ironman" will tip him off that you are the bad guy.
4. A nerd franchisee is good at some things. If he can dig through data for you, let him. Thank him for giving you the results. What data would you give him to dig through that would help both of you?
5. How can you avoid getting too chummy with a Nerd Franchisee? Getting too close can become a problem. Remember, distance is needed to keep your life out of their marvelous world.
6. What do you do when a nerd franchisee makes his store look more like him than the brand? If things get too weird at his store, call your Operations Department. The Operations Dude can run defense and keep a healthy distance for you.
7. There is no reason you need to work with someone to whom you cannot relate. Your marketing plans

do not need his OK. A nerd franchisee can operate his store on his side of town. You sell the same products and services under the same brand name. Can you tell your customers know to visit your locations? Yes!

I remember nerds from high school well and feel some of the blame for laughing when they were teased. I was young and stupid. We all were. Would there still be nerds if we did not pick on them? I have no idea. This is not that kind of book. I do, however, know I cannot change them or make them have a wonderful life. I can help them build a great business if they will listen. I am here to help and then I go home to my life and my own nerdy friends. It is the way you should be with all businesspeople. Work is work. Life starts when the time is yours to decide what to do. Now, go watch Star Wars...again.

Lesson 6

The Jock – Beer, Boobies, and Balls

Jocks are fun. They are not great franchisees, but they sure are fun.

I was short for my age or any age in high school. I love being short now that I am an adult but that was not always the case. Jocks liked to pick on different kids. Being short is different. I am sure jocks still pick on the short kids. We are like beer cans for them. We are useful for a while but, in the end, crushable. The only saving grace that kept me from becoming a nerd was that jocks can't outthink us short kids. Out-thinking them during high school was like a live action game for me and the other short kids. We could outtalk them, at least for a while. And being small, we are hard to catch. Add a little WD-40 to your clothing and you could slide through the day. Now that I think of it, wearing WD-40 may be why my high school girlfriend went to another high school.

Once jocks caught on that we were messing with them, we would be the recipients of an ATOMIC WEDGIE. I capitalized ATOMIC WEDGIE for good reason. If you have no idea what that is, I am not going to relive that memory to explain it to you. Its why we nerds created Google.

Jocks in franchises are the good-time guys of business. Where the class clowns are trying to get others to like them with jokes, jocks expected you to like them because they are, well, jocks. They were selfish and difficult to deal with when you had to work with them. Everything was a primal urge with them. They wake up thinking about beer, boobies, and sports (that is the balls in the title of this chapter).

I want you to understand that jocks in franchises are good for a while but soon get distracted. I think their selfishness comes from not being asked to think too much in high school. Everyone told them that their athletic ability would make them rich and famous. Some of them even did. They grew up as physical beings. Everything required movement to them.

For jocks in a business setting, movement gets them in trouble. Jocks in business sometimes get sued by employees for harassment because they are physical creatures. Surprisingly, jocks are shocked when it happens. They think, "So what if I move too close to a good-looking female staffer or shoulder punch a male employee while telling them they did a good job?" Jocks think everyone sees them as the hero. They were heroes in high school. Why would anyone begrudge them anything they do just because they are not still playing sports anymore and now look like they could not run up a flight of stairs if they had to? Former athletes are a mess of fun to watch at work. They are just not helpful to themselves or others in franchising.

Much like a weird science experiment, franchising and jocks have a strange symbiotic relationship. The leaders in the corporate office of some franchises feel like they spent so much time building a system that others could live off that they want to have a bunch of jocks around to talk sports and knock back a few shots of whiskey. They want to feel like they have a big tough guy around that looks up to them. The jock, for his part, wants to be part of the money team. As the outsider in their relationship, I think it looks like dysfunctional love. The franchise as a whole suffers because of it even though it is eventually going to happen. Ever heard of a professional player getting turned down for a Franchise Agreement? You will not. Trust me.

When you want to build a brand, you are going to need the guys that get things done. You just do not need a jock who thinks that moving around a store makes a good business. I can point to hundreds of businesses that failed because employees were moving and not getting anything accomplished to bring in profits. You must have the highest quality operations just like you need the highest quality products. Customers notice when people are not doing a good job and go somewhere else. A jock franchisee will not notice though. He is moving around too much to notice.

Jocks mean well. They want to be liked like they were in high school. The problem is that everyone (but them) grew up. The party ended and everyone needed to make a living. Ever wonder why marketing companies have drop-dead beautiful women in sales? Jocks buy what they are selling every single time. It is easy money.

There are jocks that do well in franchises. They do well because they have someone in the franchise watching out for them. A high-profile jock will have a business manager run the business. That means he hires someone to make the money, and he gets to go play golf or touch football. Either way, jocks in franchising can be successful if they get out of their own way and yours.

Homework #6:

If you must work with a jock, be prepared to get a wedgie...either a mental wedgie or physical wedgie.

1. If you want to make your store work with a jock franchisee nearby you need to keep him focused on a game plan. Can you find a way to treat the franchise operations as a game and each quarter of the year as a quarter in the game? Once he realizes he has something to win; he is in.

2. What would be on the list of things you need to cover in a meeting with a jock? Cover the items on your list, drink to success, and then get out. Jocks get distracted easily remember? Stick to the list!

3. Be prepared not to get anywhere in a meeting with a jock. Being distracted is a constant trend with jocks. Can you arrange another meeting? Nothing happens on Thursdays. Thursdays work for another meeting.

4. How would you create a rivalry with an opposing brand? The best jocks in business have a rival to crush. They will torment the other brand and not you!

5. Do not meet at a place with a TV, beer, hard liquor, or women not fully dressed. Nothing undermines a meeting with a jock more than their need for a party. Sports bars are not going to work for a meeting place. Where would you meet a jock to discuss business?

Extra Credit

If you want to mess with a jock, give him a challenge. The best challenge I heard about in my years as a franchise consultant was when a nerd franchisee challenged a jock franchisee to a game of "who can get more customers"

There was a big audacious promotion from the jock franchisee. There were balloons, bands, and a ribbon cutting with the mayor. The jock hired the local radio station to get customers through the door and they came!

People were interested in the freebies that the jock franchisee gave away with the company logo on it and tried out the services while they were there. It was an amazing day.

The nerd franchisee sat back and watched the promotion from his store. He put out banners and balloons but did not do much more. Customers came to his store as well. They liked the staff and the service. He invited them back and gave them a coupon for their next visit. He made a point of making the customers feel important and he remembered their names and something about them. He increased his business that day as well.

Who won the game?

They both did. The smart one in the game was the nerd. He did not spend anywhere near as much as the jock franchisee but he increased his volume. In the end, they both maintained a higher level of customers by stealing them away from the competition.

On a side note, who do you think really won?

The nerd won. He did what he could to present a great image to the customers. Service is the key. Win the customers and you win the bigger paycheck. A big event only brings customers because they like new things. Once the newness is done, customers go back to what they know and like. Make a customer feel good about your store and they will be back and bring friends.

Lesson 7

The Cheerleader Was Exhausting

Cheerleaders in high school intimated the hell out of me. I was short. Short teenagers are cute. We own the word "cute". Cute is not going to get a date with a cheerleader. OK, so we could get a date, but there would have to be alcohol and bad decisions involved. No one told me that in high school. I could have planned for that!

As for me, I only remember not being much of an athlete and thinking there was no reason to bother talking with cheerleaders. They were pretty and they always had boyfriends. That simple fact made it easier for me. I was not worried about trying to date a cheerleader or worried she would leave me for a jock. Having distance between my feelings for cheerleaders as a teen makes it easier now that I see them in franchising.

Just to start this chapter out right, please let it be known that cheerleaders have split personalities. That simple fact freaked me out when I saw it. I am surprised there are not more horror movies with cheerleaders as the villain. Cheerleaders are happy when they can lead the fun. Then, that same person can be the scariest human on earth when things are not going well for her. Smile big when you see them. It throws them off your tracks and you can give yourself space for safety.

The happy cheerleader is the one everyone thinks of when they hear "cheerleader". Cheery, smiley, fun cheerleaders make things exciting. Jocks are fun, but not like cheerleaders. Not that kind of fun. Get your mind out of the gutter. This is a business book. Jocks are looking for fun for themselves. Happy cheerleaders are looking to make you have fun. That is the point that you can work with them to grow the brand and your sales.

Energy in a business comes from the top. It is where the focus of effort comes from when the doors open for business. I tell owners all the time that what they are interested in and spend energy on with their teams will become a priority. The keys to a successful business come when teams worry about the right things. Cheerleaders thrive on energy and want you to show your enthusiasm for your work.

Cheerleaders can motivate people to move, act up, or just feel excited. When they get the right team in their franchise location, they can control an entire brand image. But, like many things, energy must be renewed or it weakens. A weak leader is worse than no leader. A tired cheerleader franchisee is freakin' scary. Cheerleaders in franchising are great when they are rooting for the right things. Did you catch that last part? When they get on the wrong track and their cheers aren't met with smiley faces they can be downright mean. Mean cheerleaders are not healthy to be around.

My job as a consultant is to make sure everyone follows the system and is making money. A cheerleader can make that difficult when she thinks she is the one leading. Cheerleaders can be brought around to the correct path. It is just a matter of finding the right cheer for them to lead.

Cheerleaders in high school brought spirit to the school. They were told to show pride in their school and make sure everyone around them showed it too. They worked hard to be the center of that attention and expected the efforts to work in their favor. Bouncing around in front of mostly guys who wanted to watch a football game made them work hard for their attention. That can be how they get tripped up in a franchise.

Franchising is not about a single franchisee. It is about the brand. Brands work when everyone blends well together. Just like jocks and nerds need to work together in a brand, a Cheerleader does as well. A cheerleader franchisee is not, nor will ever be, the center of attention. The customer is the center of attention. A cheerleader will not see that right off the bat. They want to be noticed and to make others see them as the "bringer of the spirit" of the brand. A brand is only as good as the total of all the locations selling under the brand. Just as one bad store can bring down a brand, one franchise store that is focused on the franchisee instead of the brand can ruin a legacy.

Can you imagine working for a cheerleader? Cheerleaders assume that a great attitude can bring sales and that they can inspire everyone to bring their best efforts too. Great attitudes do bring sales. That, however, does not always work with hourly employees who want to get through their shift so they can go somewhere else. What is inspiring about cleaning the public bathroom you do not own or dealing with every grumpy customer who walks through the door? Also, an hourly worker thinks he can go down the street and get another hourly job when things get tough. Self-inspiration is not an hourly trait.

Cheerleaders can have unrealistic expectations of what they can get out of employees and customers. It is what they know. I do not blame them. How many motivational speeches have you listened to over your career? How many books about being the leader have you read? The business world is filled with "You Can Do It!" style self-help tools. The best motivation is the kind that motivates you to motivate yourself. Having to fall back on a cheerleader to get you revved up again is not the answer. It is a crutch.

Want to motivate yourself?

My Dad had a great saying when I was growing up. He said, "You always find what you are looking for. If you are looking for a fight, you will find a fight. If you want money, you will find a way to earn it. What you have is what you were looking for." I never forgot that statement and I am eternally grateful that he gave me that advice. Dads are good for that. They are not good cheerleaders, but they do get you moving.

Homework #7:

To deal with a Cheerleader Franchisee you need to smile really, really big at her and then re-direct the conversation.

- Getting a cheerleader to listen to you is not hard. Getting her to cheer for the right things is. Ask a cheerleader to help you motivate the rest of the franchisees forward by following the system. Once she feels useful, she will follow along.
- Working near a cheerleader franchisee is exhausting! Think of her as a power plant that you need to be careful around that can charge you up or blow you up.
- Check her cheery message often. A cheerleader franchisee wants to be creative. Writing on windows and changing the look of the franchise store can go against the Franchise Agreement and move them away from cheering for the right things.
- Check the cheerleader franchisee's level of energy (remember the power plant analogy?). No one can be energetic all the time and the brand suffers when she is tired. Faking cheeriness with customers and employees gives the wrong message. Give her time to reenergize. Help a cheerleader franchisee hire cheery people.
- Watch out that your employees do not get caught-up in her happy ways. You will have to add some of her motivational cheers to your leadership routine

to keep them on your team. She can steal good employees by making her store look like a happier place to work than yours.

- When she gets worn out and cannot find another person to cheer up, she will want to sell. Be ready to buy. There is nothing wrong with developing a good business relationship with someone who is going to get tired and look for a new group to cheer up.

Extra Credit

Go watch a game. Make sure it's a game with cheerleaders. They spend a lot of energy on trying to whip the crowd into a frenzied state. Turn around and watch the audience and see if anyone really notices the cheerleaders. Does it whip them into doing anything?

Nope.

So, why are there cheerleaders? Answer that and you will know where a cheerleader needs to be in your business.

Write your answer in the form of a 5-page essay. It is due tomorrow.

Lesson 8

The Kid Everyone Knew But No One Knew Anything About

If you have ever worked in an office, you know there is one person; at least one person, whom everyone knows but no one can tell you anything about him or her. That person started out as a shy kid in high school and grew into being the shadow of everyone else. There is nothing creepy or insidious about this person. He is just like the walls – there, but not noticed unless someone wants to make a change. You see a painting on a wall before you see the wall. That is the same for this guy. He is just behind the scenes. He is also making changes to make sure you do not see him. He is smart, creative, and alone.

For a kid that everyone (and no one) knows, you will waste all sorts of energy trying to get him to do more, be the leader, or be goal driven. In high school, he was smart but not an honor student. He kept things just under the radar so he would not be picked on by the teacher for answers or the other students for being different.

Please do not mistake this guy for being stupid. He is strategically smart and can manipulate situations to disappear. Be careful to keep that in mind. He may be smarter than you. He just does not like to be seen. He is also a master of being there when you do not know it. He is a great intelligence gatherer. It keeps him ready to move when the spotlight is about to be shined in his direction.

High school was not rough on him other than being another day on the planet that he survived. He is not interested in being the best, not that he is defective or in need of something. In fact, he does not need anything. He is a creature unlike most people. He can make do with anything or nothing. In high school, everyone wanted to be the person with the latest fashions and stuff. No kid wanted to be a standout for the wrong reason, unless you were the kid everyone (and no one) knew. He did not care and after getting teased a couple of times without fighting back or getting upset about it, the student body just left him alone. And that was what he wanted. This is his ultimate strategy.

In a franchise, the guy everyone knows but no one knows anything about is kind of a pain in the neck to work with. He spent so much time alone that being a part of a brand is the opposite of what he is used to. Why would he join a franchise? The simple answer is that he does not have to be the guy to talk with vendors or figure out the marketing plan. Working for himself allows him to be ignored when he does an excellent job setting the system to run without him. He does not have to stand out if he hires a good manager and staff. He is just there in the background trying to manipulate things. OK, so now it is starting to sound creepy.

When you are the owner, you are the CEO of your business. Most CEOs need to be seen and heard from to make sure the employees are following the owner's vision for the company and the franchise system. He sets the system and deals as little as possible with people inside his store and inside the brand. He is a shadow in the brand. Not that he is going to hurt the brand since that would bring attention to him, but he is not going to be the best or win awards. That is unless there is an award for being amazingly average.

On the positive side of things, he is going to follow the rules. I like that in a franchisee. I will not have to spend much time checking to make sure he is compliant with the brand requirements. He is going to follow along and find a happy medium to get everything done and not be the first to finish or the last. The guy everyone knows but no one knows anything about is known for nothing. Consistency in business is a great thing. Customers can latch onto places that they know the service and the products will be the same every time. Money can be made year after year with a consistent approach.

The franchisee everyone knows but no one knows anything about will be the one that employees try walk all over to get what they want. He is not seen around his own business and he doesn't make a scene. That makes him a target. But the employees are sadly mistaken. If you try to make a scene with someone who owns the business and does not want a scene, he will move you away from his business quickly. He is not good at asking for help. He does not need help. He is self-sufficient and can keep his business going until it is burned down or gets too popular. Either way, he is going to make the situation better to get back to normal.

As a franchisee who is dealing with a guy everyone knows but no one knows anything about, you should be aware of this shy, smart, manipulative personality near you. The one thing you should not do is bring too much attention to his business. You can run rings around his operations and he is not going to approach you to work with you. He is going to give customers only what they want and then he will disappear. He will show up for franchise meetings if they are required, but he is not going to participate. He is happy to let everyone else fight it out.

Homework #8:

1. The kid everyone knew but no one knew anything about is a shadow and that makes him almost impossible to work with. How can he be invisible and still help your brand?
2. He is an information gatherer. It keeps him from being picked on. It also is vital information for you and your business. If he is unwilling to go after customers directly, he is still finding customers. That undercurrent of customer growth is the lifeblood of a business. Can you ask him what he does to bring in customers and get a real answer?
3. If a guy everyone knows but no one knows anything about in a franchise is determined to keep a low profile, he may try to keep you down too if you are bringing too much attention to the brand. You can insulate your stores from his by labeling your stores in your advertising. What would you advertise to keep customers from confusing your business with his?
4. The guy everyone knows and no one knows anything about franchisee may try to avoid using event marketing that is required by the franchisor if it draws too much attention to his business. Who would you contact to get him to follow the brand system even if he can't hide?
5. He will need a strong manager. Help him find a good manager. If that sounds wrong since you would be helping someone else make money,

think about having to deal with a store near yours in the same brand that has a rotten manager. Customers see a brand name, not an individual franchise. The cost of bringing back a customer who had a bad experience is much higher than helping a franchise near yours run better.

Lesson 9

That Damn Bully

Every high school and every business has a bully. There are not any exterminators who can handle ridding us of this kind of pest. We deal with the annoyance this guy brings and know it is coming back again to drive us nuts. Why are there bullies? It is God's way of reminding us not to get too comfortable with our lunch money. Wet willies, Atomic Wedgies, Swirlies all sound like great bar drinks but are the stuff of nightmares when you are a freshman in high school. OK, so God may not have anything to do with bullies. It's probably the other guy with the fire and pitchfork. Either way, we are reminded why we hated high school when we have to stand face-to-face with a guy "hell-bent" on making our lives miserable.

What created a bully in school? It could be that he was bigger than the other kids and he was intimidating. It could be that he was the weird kid that fought back and won. It could be that mutants had a baby and sent him to school. In any case, he is not nice and he is not someone anyone wants to be around. He is tolerated if he is on a sports team because he intimidates the other team but once he leaves the field, everyone is glad he is gone. He learned to be a pain in the seated parts to get what he wants and now, as an adult, that is how he leads his life every day.

In business, a bully is the guy who pushes you to the point where you decide whether you want to throw in the towel or fight back. You know a bully acts like he has nothing to lose even when he does. If you are the unluckiest of souls, he is your boss. He was nice when you came in but makes life a mess when you must get work done. He takes pride in creating chaos for you to deal with and clean up. Treating him as a poisonous lizard is not a bad idea since, well, he is.

In a franchise, a bully is the guy who got in with a smile and a scam. He is there to drive other franchisees out of business and snatch up their franchise stores as fast as he can for as little as he can possible pay. He is not there to be anyone's friend since he already knows he is hated. He is in it for his own selfish pursuits and doesn't give a damn about the brand. He will fight with anyone.

God bless anyone anywhere around him. They tolerate a mess of a person and the worst of environments in which to work. So, what can you do to make things work well when you have a bully for a brand partner? The answer is not to be nice to him or to reason with him. Both ways will just egg him on and you'll end up with egg on your face...possibly real egg. A smart franchisee knows that to work with a bully, you need to work against him. How in the world do you work against someone who only wants to annoy and destroy you? It is the same answer the teacher had when she had to deal with the bully. Something needs to be a bigger threat to the bully than the reward of hurting you. Your teachers understood this dynamic and even used it on you when you were acting up.

For a bully franchisee, his focus is on all ideas to create chaos. When it comes to building a strong business, they are lost. Your job is to hurt him by driving customers to your store. A price cut for a couple of weeks can be enough of a hurting. Since he is not good at customer service, he is going to lose that numbers game. More customers through your doors equal more profits even with lower margins.

The "numbers game" is what is played every day in business. You need to have enough customers to more than breakeven and you can weather a storm. Coupons, advertised price cuts, and extra offerings push customers into your store. It will send customers into his store as well. The difference is that customers to his store will not come back. When he starts losing customers, he is going to blame someone instead of re-examining his operations. That is the start of his sled ride down the slippery slope of failure.

Can it really be that easy? Yes, maybe. Sometimes bullies implode on their own broken merits. On the other hand, some bullies are smarter than that and save their sorry hides with deals of their own. The best bet is to pay attention to the number of customers you have and work to double that number. Doubling is a strategy that is easy for your entire team to work with and embrace. Making your franchise location the go-to place for customers is your first and best priority.

The other tactic is to redirect the bully to something more of a target than you. Magicians and teachers use redirection to make things disappear. You can disappear from a bully's sight if you plan for it. The first step to redirecting the bully is to make something more important than you. Once he is focused on something else, take that time to grow your business quickly.

A good target that he will go after is your biggest competition. It is a natural enemy. He bought a brand and a logo. It is already in his mind as a target. Use that idea to force him to work hard to push the competition out of business. You can already see how this can be a win-win.

I worked with a bully franchisee who liked to order the other franchisees around and make them pay for the marketing plans he created. He, of course, was the one getting the most out of the marketing. He was a classic bully and was always looking to pit franchisees against each other to see them fight. I found out that he had a competitor nearby that lost its manager and "innocently" mentioned it to him. He spent the next month and a half sending bad workers into his store to ask for an application to be manager. The owner of that store eventually hired one of those workers and nearly went out of business. The poor manager the competitor hired destroyed the brand image at that location and the owner lost almost every customer. Once you start down a slippery slope with poor customer service, it is hard to recover. Eventually, that location closed. I feel bad for the owner but he made the choice on whom to hire. He could have waited for a better manager. Bullies create situations where what they want you to pick is the best in a bad lineup of choices. It is a great strategy for a manipulator. Never assume that everything is just happening or that it is fate. Sometimes, there is a bully at the end of it pulling strings to make your life miserable.

Damn bullies!

Homework #9:

1. If you have a bully in your franchise, look for ways to move his focus to something you can control. Is there a competitor that you can sic him on?

2. Bully franchisees are looking for weakness. Take the time to find your own weaknesses. Make a list of areas you need to work on and then fix them.

3. If a bully franchisee sees you as a target, make every effort to bring in the franchisor to assist. As a Franchise Consultant, I can make him very uncomfortable by just forcing him to follow the franchise system. In what situation do you think you should call your franchisor for help?

4. There is no reasoning with a bully. Stop trying. The best you can do is to limit his access to your business. Do you have a policy to keep your employees from divulging your business statistics? Write a security policy into your Employee Manual.

5. Bullies are people too. No, not nice people, but they are human. They have insecurities just like you do. The difference is that they do not like anyone to know and will cause you an immense amount of grief if they know you found out. How can you keep an eye on a bully, but leave room too?

6. How can you keep a distance from a bully franchisee down the street? The same way you hid from the crazy date you had that kept coming around, find ways to not be available to meet with the bully. Brainstorm ways to be busy in an instant.

Lesson 10

Teachers Are People Too

Yes, there are teachers in franchising. You did not join something that you already knew how to operate. If you knew everything, you would have done it on your own. In franchising, teachers are the trainers both in the classroom and in the field. Franchisors label them as training managers or specialists, educators, or the operations team. I would add the executives as teachers, but they have their own function in a franchise and rarely make an appearance to teach anything. Some do, but overall, they have something else to work on other than to teach a franchisee how to be profitable. We will talk about executives in the next chapter. Just wait!

Teachers are on the other side of franchising from franchisees. Teachers have the fun task of trying to get the information from the Operations Manual out of the book, into your head, and then into practice in the stores. There must be something in the DNA of a teacher that makes doing this job interesting to them because dealing with adult learners is borderline psychotic. If you think your high school teacher went through a lot trying to get you to remember when the Sedition Act was passed by Congress, you haven't seen anything like a room full of adults trying to think like franchisees. God bless all teachers. God bless them all.

If you are someone who is successful in another industry, you probably think you will be successful in franchising. That is a lie you are telling yourself. If you were CEO or Vice President of a multi-national conglomerate, that does not mean you can handle a dozen hourly employees well. It is two vastly different groups. You may wield power as a highly paid executive, but as for being the boss of a group that barely made it out of high school and can get another job in the same strip center as your store; you are grapes for them to stomp on. Now, take that executive and put him into a classroom full of people who are just like him, and they all now have to listen and learn and follow rules. Not that they will not succeed, but they are going to fail for a while before they remember how to learn and follow rules like they did in high school. God bless all teachers.

In high school, teachers were given a stack of information that you, the student, had to learn in order to pass to get to the next grade and eventually graduate. High school teachers are not given enough credit for getting a bunch of hormone crazed, "I stayed up all last night talking on the phone to my girlfriend/boyfriend" and "I want to be somewhere else" kids to sit still. Getting actual information into a student's head long enough to take a test is a miracle. God bless all teachers.

Now that you are all grown up, you would think that being in a classroom that you paid hard-earned money to be in would be a different story. It should be a room full of gracious, intelligent people all looking for answers on how to run a great store and looking forward to opening many new stores. Instead, you get a bunch of people who are playing on their Iphones and wanting to be somewhere else. Nothing changes after high school. Everyone learned how to act in a classroom when they were still wondering how many days it was until summer vacation. The secret is that your teachers had a chart that listed the number of days until summer vacation too. The great big secret we do not tell you until it is too late is: There are no summer breaks in franchising. God bless all teachers.

In the franchise field, teachers just get beat up. I am an operations expert. Sometimes, I am required to bring bad news to a franchisee. Since I am in the field, I will spend time face-to-face with a franchisee. And that is when I get in trouble. I have been stabbed and shot at trying to give information to franchisees that they did not want to hear. It was not on the same day, but it happened in my career in the field playing the role of teacher. No, I am not exaggerating. This is not a job for someone who thinks he can just leave at five o'clock. God bless all teachers.

Franchisees think that the operations team is there to answer questions and get out of the way. The operations team is looked at as a kind of human version of an online search engine. Ask the question and in split second we will shoot out an answer for you. This is another lie. We must be on top of our game and ready with an answer that helps you at all times, but I have a life outside of your business too. I do not have to answer my phone on my vacation. You need to learn your lessons and do things by the book. Most answers are in the Operations Manual. Just like textbooks in high school, you have to start your search in the Operations Manual. God bless all teachers.

The biggest problem we in the field have is that we still need to get the information into the franchisee's head and then into practice. We cannot get out of the way. You made us your partner when you signed your Franchise Agreement. That also does not mean that I work for you. Yes, I can run your store, but I am not going to. I do not work for you. You do not pay me. Your royalties pay for your right to use the system. I am here to help you stay out of trouble and keep you on track. I do not clean bathrooms, and I am not on your schedule to work a shift. This will make you mad and disgruntled. How can I just let you do all the heavy lifting when I am an expert in operations? It is your store, and I have a bunch of franchisees just like you wanting all my time. I cannot be there for you all the time. Learn your lessons. Learn where you can find answers and leave me as a final call for help. I can teach you. But, if I taught you the same lesson for the hundredth time and you keep calling me, I am not going to be a happy teacher. God bless all teachers.

You may have already put together that I am one of those insane people who love doing this kind of work. Teaching is the ultimate leadership position. It is a job that requires long hours and time away from home. It is a thankless job, and if done well, is overlooked often when awards are given out. Why would I spend a career doing this? Is it in my DNA? Probably, since I keep coming back to it. None of us who do this for living take it lightly. Once you have had a shotgun aimed at your back while you are running out of a store, you get a little cautious about teaching lessons easily. Even if it is helpful to the franchisee, I still do not give advice the way reasonable person would. Remember, I already know you are unbalanced. You bought a franchise and started talking about making lots of money. You are going to be treated as a hormonal nut job for a while.

Teachers who work in the field must find a balance between getting information to the franchisee, being the designated thug when needed, and act as a bartender to listen to all the franchisee's problems. This is not a job for an emotionally weak person. God bless all teachers.

Teaching franchisees has become a game of small wins for me. I am sure high school teachers are like this too. Franchisees have a lot on their plate before they even get out of bed in the morning. When I show up, I am adding to that pile. Not only am I grading them on their operations, but I am required to enforce the rules of the franchise. Teaching is in there, but some days, it takes a while for the lesson to be learned. It is a system of breaking down the big goals into small wins that you can celebrate and build on. It is the same thing your parents did with you when you were small and your teachers did in high school. The more you did right, the more you wanted to do right because you were getting a mini celebration every time you did. God bless all teachers.

High school teachers must have compositions of steel nerves and iron will. They definitely do not get paid what they are worth. There are women in my family (my Momma, my sister and my sister-in-law) who are teachers and what they go through to teach students is not equal to their pay. Not fair, but they keep teaching. It's in their DNA. Plus, summers off is a bonus most of us do not get. I do not begrudge them the summer off. I think I'd rather do my own dental surgery rather than be in a classroom full of teenagers everyday for a school year. God bless all teachers.

As for the teachers in franchising:

- Teachers should level the playing field as fast as possible. It is a team sport and franchisees and franchisors are both on the same team. When one side thinks it has the upper hand, nothing works. That includes franchisors who think they can walk on franchisees. Great teachers show respect and authority and make life super hard when you do not make the grade.

- All teaching should be pointed toward a goal. If you want to make more money, make sure you let everyone know that is the lesson. If you want to hire better employees, make sure you aim the conversations toward recruiting. Do not get off topic...for long.
- You, as the franchisee, know your strengths and weaknesses better than the operations team. At least, you should know them better than us. Tell us what you are weak in and we will teach you or find someone who can help you learn. Hiding weaknesses didn't work in high school and it means your competitor can kick your butt. When customers see that you are weak in something, you lose. Ask the teacher for help.
- Be nice to all teachers. You didn't care for your teachers in high school but now you are older and can appreciate that someone is trying to help you grow. Quit trying to be right all of the time and thank them.
- Teachers are tired and can be cranky like you are sometimes. They are human and can have bad days too. Do not be a dork and hold it against them. If you put a wedge in the middle of your relationship with your teacher, you have a long road back to the level playing field.
- Teachers can also be the designated thugs of the franchise world. Enforcement can be a big hammer against you if you are not working well together.

Remember getting in trouble in high school? You have more to lose now.

- You put money into something that can either drain your financial accounts or help you retire sooner. If you will not learn and see that everyone loses when you lose, then sell and go be a great employee for someone else.

God bless all teachers in the world. They do a thankless job and are forgotten fast. The best lesson I ever learned was when I had to teach a group of franchisees and realized how tiring it is to be the "lightning rod" in the room. All the energy is directed at you and then drained out of you. Being a parent is similar, but not exactly like being a teacher. You can ground your own kids. Try that on someone else's kid and the police will visit with you. Try that with a franchisee and you get sued. Just once I want you to try to keep a room full of "know-it-all's" attention long enough to get a lesson taught. You will seek out and hug your homeroom teacher from high school.

God bless all teachers.

Lesson 11

Guidance Counselors Don't Use GPS

I remember my Guidance Counselor as a nice lady who didn't help me at all. She gave me a test to see what I was good at and said I could be a great assistant somewhere...or a doctor. That worried me. What the heck kind of test says I can do grunt work or hold a person's life in my hands? She apparently did not work that hard to keep her job. Although, for a split second, the experience did make me want her job, I could not get over the fact that she was messing with me. Everyone messes with you in high school; why wouldn't the Guidance Councilor? My guidance counselor is somewhere in the world not remembering me at all. That, at least, is my expectation for her.

Being a counselor to high schoolers must be frustrating. I wonder if there is an automatic link with how fast the student's eyes roll when a guidance councilor says the word "future". As in, "If you do not buckle down and study, you are not going to have much of a future." I bet it is measured in milliseconds. An upperclassman can sense when an adult is going to ask them to do something and start looking skyward without moving his head. Measuring that would have been a better experiment than dissecting a frog.

In franchising, the Operations Department is the guidance counselors. Data on every part of the business is one key to growth in franchising. We test you and give you the news of how you are faring in business. Yes, we are going to tell you to buckle down and work harder. And yes you are going to roll your eyes at us. It is funny how eye rolling comes back to you right when you need it. It is also weird that I turn into my dad when someone rolls his eyes at me when I am talking. The tough part is that I cannot take away TV privileges when a franchisee gets smarmy at me. (Smarmy is a real word.)

Guidance counselors analyze your permanent records (did I see a full body shiver when you saw "permanent record" in this chapter?) and figure out what you are good at doing and what you need help with. That is what we, on the corporate team, are always trying to do for you too. Just like high school, more often than not, you are going to resist listening to good advice. After all, who am I to tell you how to run your business or your life? Business and life are far too intertwined for common sense to jump to the top of rational thought. And, because of that, you push back and resist doing the things that will help you succeed. In fact, pushing back hard against advice seems to be the standard working model for franchisees. It worked in high school didn't it?

Guidance counselors are like teachers without giving you a deadline for getting your homework done. They are usually seen when you are in trouble or in need of someone to get you on track to the next part of your adventure. High school guidance counselors want you to go to college. They are not bonused on how many students get into college, but they should be. How many more people would be better educated if there was someone at your school whose pay depended on you making it to the next grade?

In franchising, either the operations department or the entire corporation is bonused on how the franchisees do. That is a big factor in why I am a pain in your ass and getting all up in your business. I want my paycheck! I also want to see you succeed. OK, so I want my paycheck more than I want your success, but it's an amazingly close second. Really! After all, I am a consultant. All I have is my reputation and a laptop. Sometimes my laptop works, but I always need my reputation as a great consultant. And I am only great when you are great. Do you think you have it rough as a franchisee? Try having your reputation tied to how franchisees do at operating their business. Being a franchise consultant is like being a rodeo clown. You are not the star and you get a lot of bull when and where you do not need it. At least I do not have to dress like a clown…most of the time. Although, there was one time… Hmm, maybe I'll save that for another book.

Guidance Counselors are like hockey goalies. They give you a swift (metaphorical) hit and get you back in the game. They do not make plays, and they do not score the winning goal. They do, however, keep the game moving and the players in action. They do not sit with you to make sure you do your job and they do not care if you skip school. They are there when you need them and you only need them to meet a requirement to graduate. No wonder my counselor was so bad at what she did. There was no reason to try harder.

When you need to work with a Guidance Counselor:

- Why would you need to deal with a high school guidance counselor again? You graduated from high school and will never have to go back. Of course, a guidance counselor in franchising is going to show you ways to make money. That should make you listen.
- If you work with a guidance counselor, be nice. He probably just got the bull's horns from the last franchisee he met with that day.
- Guidance counselors in a franchise want to help you and are tied to your success. Push them for more ideas and what stories they can tell you of other franchisees who are succeeding. Write down what they tell you. Something may not work now but it could make the difference later.
- Ask questions! The thing I did not do when I was in high school was to engage my guidance counselor. You would be reading a much better book if I had. It would not be nearly as fun, but it would have loftier thinking. They have resources that you can use. Ask!

- Good counselors help show you what is around the next turn. Any good franchise is looking for change to keep them ahead of the competition. Find out what your franchise is looking at doing in the next year. Offer to test things. Start up fees can be waived and training is covered by the corporate office.
- Now, write an essay on what lessons you have learned so far in the book. I have plenty of red pens to make notes for you and grade your perception of what it takes to be a good franchisee. Yeah, I use old school red pens!

Lesson 12

The Principal Had Better Things to Do

Of all the people in high school, the principal had the most visible job and never seem to be doing anything important. It is not true, but it did seem that way. The best leaders in a high school are working behind the scenes to ensure things keep running smoothly and that they do not look like they are sweating the small stuff.

I had great administrators in high school. No, I was not on a first name basis with them, but my brothers were well known by them. Ha! My siblings only thought they could get out of being called out in my book. I have two older brothers who I think of as great, weird guys. (I said great first). They are one and two years older than me and that was a problem in high school. By the time I came to be a freshman, teachers had that worn out look on their faces when they read my name. The first day of class I was asked if I was going to be like my brothers in class. I never knew how to answer that question correctly. Either I could be honest and say yes, I am a trouble-maker like my brothers or I can lie and let the teachers find out on their own. I went with the lie. Getting labeled as trouble from day-one took a lot longer to survive than to let the teacher figure it out.

I have a younger brother and two younger sisters. There is a five-year gap between me and my younger brother. They went to high school in a different town. They got the opportunity to create their own reputations. It does come down to location, location, location after all, doesn't it?

Getting back to the high school administration, the principal is the backbone of the system. If you have a slacker principal, you have slacker teachers. If you have a thunderous, hard-nosed principal, you have a school that has fearful teachers and students. Yes, there is learning in both places, but neither leadership style is good for helping build successful students.

How many of you had a principal like that?

I can tell you that I had a different kind of principal. She was great at doing the big things and the small things. She knew what was happening and when to step in. No, she was not liked as many of the teachers were, but we knew the school had rules and what happened when we stepped out of line. Great leaders do that well. Setting expectations is the name of the game. If you know what will happen if you set fire to the chemistry lab or start a fight in the gymnasium, you are likely not to follow that path. You saw the principal when you needed to and when the expectations changed. Principals are not teachers. They are the path setters. If you do not like it, get homeschooled.

In a franchise, the principal is the president. The president of a franchise is the most visible high ranking leader and usually gets the blame for everything that goes wrong.

The "principal president" is not there to handle your small problems like finding new employees or dealing with vendors unless it is a system-wide problem that needs a stronger voice. He is there to make sure you know what is expected of you and where the company is going. He creates change and monitors the system. You see him when you need to see him and not before or after the fact. He is the first and last to speak. It is like being the captain on a cruise ship. No need to see him as long as the boat is still floating along where you want it to go.

The principal president is also the person that can be left out of local changes if they are not keeping a close eye on things. They assume a lot of things and get crazy mad when they find out problems after the fact. They deal with vice-presidents and others who want their job, so there is a bit of strategy that gets played against them on a daily basis. It is not an easy job.

If you were the person who had to announce changes to a group of people who are all thinking that they haven't seen you in a year and that you do not know their business at all, you are going to get a wide range of reactions. Imagine standing in front of several thousand people and telling them they are required to spend profits on a new cash register or a new menu board. It won't increase sales or drive in more customers, but upgrades are a part of the deal when you are in business. The difference between independent owners and franchisees is the look of the store. Over time, nothing changes at the independent business. The franchise store gets updates often because the Principal see things with fresh eyes. It does make a difference to customers, but not fast enough for owners.

Want to know how a franchise president earns his pay? Tell a group of franchisees who are losing money that things will get better. I like to duck out of the room when that speech starts. It gets ugly fast. No stand-up comic could handle the heckling a president gets. They would quit and go back to being a barista for a living.

Dealing with the principal president is either good or bad. There is not a middle ground with him. If you are doing everything you need to, you are invisible to him. If you are pushing too hard or not trying hard enough, you are a target for his attention. Again, that is either good or bad. It depends on how he sees you.

- Ask answerable questions of the principal president. If he can give you an answer that makes him look and feel good, you are now on his radar in a good way. Ask what the hell he was thinking when he made a decision, and you will find a new level of pain.
- Treat the principal president as you would your grandparent. Yes, he is wise and can give you advice, but he is tired, and you will wear him out

fast. The entire chain is asking him to help. It ain't just you doing the asking.

- Be aware that he has minions listening for him. No principal president is alone in the room. He is going to have the rest of the group tell him what he missed. Their opinion is what makes the basis of his liking or hating you.
- Do not expect him to give you an answer when you ask the question. He is wary of doing that since he has been burned by answering too fast in his past. Also, do not expect him to act on even the best ideas in a timely manner. He is going to create a committee to study an idea. And then, there is testing and then there is a beta version, and then finally, it gets rolled out to the system. By then, you have sold your stores. It is called the "Two Year Rule". From the time you mention an idea until it gets rolled out, two years have passed and he can then call it his idea.
- Anything he tells you when he is drinking is meaningless. Even if he promises you something small, it does not matter. He will tell you that you misunderstood him. It is like a mulligan for franchise leaders. If there is a drink in his hand, nothing counts. Enjoy your free drink and leave before he does.
- The Principal President is the one who gets the final say. Even if he is wrong, do not waste your time hounding him. He is not going to change his

mind. He looks weak if he flip-flops. Get over it or he will get over you.

- Thank him for his leadership and smile. He gets enough scowls. Just like a customer, you need him to be friendly back to you, so be friendly first.

Lesson 13

Cliques – You're Not Being as Cool as You Remember

Oh man, there were there cliques when we were in high school. There were big cliques, and ones you did not want to join and then there were the ones you wanted badly to be a part of but couldn't. I think it is a requirement that you fall into a clique that will label you forever. No one tells you that you cannot swap cliques. No one did, did they? It is like the mafia. Once you are in, you are there for life. Get used to it and make the best of it.

Everyone remembers high school in a different way. Most people think of it as a movie that plays in their head and is fuzzy around the edges. The bad stuff that happened back then seems worse and the good stuff is amazing. The fuzzy edges of your memory just focus your thoughts on how you saw it. The people that were around you when the worst and best parts of your teen years happened see it differently and probably do not remember anything that happened to you. Sorry, but they remember the best and worst of their own experiences. You were not in their movie.

Cliques are the exception to that rule. Cliques make it so that you had experiences with other people and then talked about it and agreed to what really happened, whether it really did or not. Have you ever listened to people talk about high school? There is no way someone fit into a locker and stayed there all weekend. My locker was too small for all my books let alone a person. And I'm small enough to fit into a suitcase! Someone's Mom would have had the police and a news crew at the school to find a student jammed into a locker.

Cliques made you feel like you had a space in the world where someone had your back and you could breathe. Life is too short to not belong somewhere. Cliques are also the places where you found out that no one is in charge, everyone is picked on and someone is going to find out your secrets and keep them forever. OK, so the secrets are something they will pull out every time they see you, but they keep them to share them on those special occasions.

Life in a clique makes you belong. Life in a Franchise Clique is the same way. A franchise in itself is a clique. If you listen to rival brands, you would think there is going to be a rumble in the parking lot after the big game. Franchise brands sound just like rival high schools. "You suck!" and "You cannot beat us! We are number one!" gets trotted out just like the state championship is at stake. It always makes me laugh. They sound just like their kids.

Do cliques help? Yes and no. Cliques are a starting point when you start high school. In high school, you never leave a clique. You didn't want to leave the safety of your clique and they wouldn't let you. If you learned to deal with people effectively, you could have been an effective member of any group and bounce between them. With the help of this book, you can deal with all those people you meet no matter what clique they are inside of your franchise. And you can look cooler than you thought you were in high school.

Break down cliques into the bases:

- Cliques are for finding and working with people who have similar interests. I would say that any franchise is its own clique. You want a strong brand leader and to make as much money as you can with the least amount of work.
- Cliques are for getting consensus. You bring an idea and bounce it off the other members of the clique. If it matches the group's ideology, then you do it. Anyone not agreeing with the group gets voted down. Cliques sound democratic!
- The problem with cliques is that groupthink tends to keep the group from making changes. Business is change and unless you are willing to reach out for new ideas and ways of getting in front of new customers, you will be eaten up by the competition.
- Cliques that are not aligned with the brand will destroy the brand. You may notice limits on how many franchise locations you can buy (if you sit down and read your Franchise Agreement). That is to keep a large group from voting against the owners of the franchise or the board of directors.

Working with a clique that you are not in requires that you have someone who can vouch for you. That person doesn't need to be a high-ranking member of the clique. You just need someone to see things your way enough to want to bring you in for a meeting. As a franchise consultant, I am always looking for cliques and who can help me get a foot in the door, so to speak. My best tool for motivating a group is my reputation. Having someone who is liked in the clique vouch for me is critical.

For you as a franchisee, you will need to work with them, so find a friendly face and start a small conversation.

- Ask enough questions to learn what the group thinks about the franchise and the people running the corporation. Even bad news from the clique helps you know what buttons to push and what to avoid.
- Be prepared to be scrutinized as a business owner. The clique is looking to see if you can help them. Yes, they want to use you. But, you are looking for them for help too, so it all evens out.
- After meeting with a clique, do a quick ROI (return on your investment). How much time will you need to spend to get them to help you with marketing, promotions, influencing the franchisor, etc? If you see that the time and energy spent working with them is more than what it would cost you do to the work on your own, or that they wouldn't impact

you enough to warrant working with them, then do not.

No one said that dealing with franchisees was easy. At least no one I know would say that. A clique gives you leverage to see people as a group. Once you know what leaning they have toward marketing or any other function in a franchise, tap them for help or leave them alone.

Lesson 14

Ugh! Homework!

Did you think you were done with homework when you left school? Anyone with kids knows that you get the "wonderful opportunity" to go back through school when your kids bring their homework to you with a problem they cannot solve. My son hit fifth grade, and I stopped remembering how to figure out answers to his questions. No wonder there is a show poking fun at us over the age of eleven. I tell him I need him to learn to find the answers for himself. Yes, it is a cop out. No, I do not feel guilty about it. In the pursuit of keeping my dignity intact, I refuse to put myself through the struggle to do math with letters in it. I bet the snarky smart kids are the teachers now.

In high school, homework was the burden you had to bear to get a good grade or, at least, get your parents off your back for a little while. The smart kids thought homework was fun. What did they know? They were not even trying to have a social life. Homework was the stuff that makes regular kids crazy. We all wanted to do the job and be done with it. Or, at least we want to be able to have done enough to end the day on a high note.

Homework is like that snotty little brother who will not leave you alone (Luckily, I have a great little brother. I am not just saying that because he's bigger than me now. He is and has always been a good guy). Homework, like a sugared-up kid who thinks he should be right beside you all day long, invades your personal space and makes you work when you want to sit still and eat pizza or whatever you do when you are not working. It nags at you and keeps you thinking about it until you respond. Homework is a pain, but it is there and if you ignore it too long, someone is going to ground you in ways you do not want to learn about.

Homework in high school just got in the way. It was boring most of the time and seemed to only give the teachers a way of punishing you for being in their class. I overheard a couple of my teachers talking about homework in the hallway one time during high school. They were laughing (teachers laughed? Who knew?) as well as talking about how much homework they gave us. They loved the fact that we were burdened with research and writing a paper. Not being one to let someone get the upper hand on me, I stepped forward and reminded them that they had to grade each and every paper that was turned in. From my little stand I got extra work and got an extra paper to write. There is something to be said for shutting your mouth and just letting others feel like they won.

The homework you have in franchising is bigger and more involved than you ever thought you would have to deal with when you signed your Agreement. You have payroll, royalties, advertising fees, taxes, hiring/ firing paperwork, insurance, bills, and customer feedback. That just gets you started on the homework you need to research and have a paper trail to keep you in line and give you tracking. The paper trail these days can be spreadsheets in your computer, but if you do not keep up with it, you will fail - just like in high school.

The differences between failing in high school and failing in business are monumental. In high school, you get a chance to redo an entire grade if you just give up on homework. If you give up in business, you can lose everything and even go to jail. The government (the snotty big brother) takes it hard when you do not play well with them and pay your taxes.

I bet the guy who sold you on getting into a franchise never mentioned all the paperwork you would have to do. He was smooth talking about you being your own boss and having the freedom to do what you wanted when you wanted to do it. Not once did he stop and say that you better keep good records or you will get zapped like a moth at a bug light on a hot summer night if you get audited. He probably missed that you will be sued by all your employees if you do not process your payroll and get checks to them when you promised. Homework never ends. It just gets uglier when you do not do it right.

As for being your own boss, that is a myth that I will discuss in another book. You trade one boss for another "boss" when you become a franchisee or independent business owner. The time you get to yourself happens when you have a fully trained staff, vendors who get you what you need on time, and a CPA and bookkeeper who know your business and can do some of the paperwork for you. Get over the fact that you bought something that someone called "turnkey". Your business is not just going to make money for you. You have to work at it. That was part of what high school was trying to teach you. Put the work in so you can have the time to relax. Work comes first.

Let's all be honest. Homework sucks. It is a necessity of life. The people who are good at doing the research into what is working and not working in their business will succeed. If you do not know what is going on in your own business, you are in for a rude (and I mean RUDE) awakening. Business is a series of actions, trends, and reactions. You need to make something happen, track the progress, and then react to what the trends tell you. Missing a week of data can sink a business. Great owners read the data and the trends like a book. It is the story of their business. What does the story of your actions tell you? Have you tracked them? Do you not think you should?

Let's break your homework down into neat piles.

Marketing

- Are their times of the year, month, or week when sales jump naturally? What do you do to maximize those sales?

- The action would be to find the natural trends and advertise for more customers just before those times.
- The trends would be the increase in sales during the promotion as compared to the prior few weeks or months or the prior year's sales.
- Finally, the reaction would be to make any changes needed to get more customers and sales during that time next year and during future promotions in the same year.

- What have you trained your employees to do during a promotion? Do they know what to do, how to do it, and do they want to do it?
  - Training is an action that gets cut first during slow times when it should be the first thing to ramp up when you start losing business.
  - The trends are listed in how much more the employees sell during a promotion. If you cannot tell who sold something, you need to change the way you ring up sales.
  - The reaction is in training some more. Just because your team acted well or poorly does not mean that it is 100% their fault. Did you really check to see if they understood what you wanted and that they wanted to give you 100%?

Paying Bills

Taking care of payroll, vendor invoices, insurance, rent, and everything else that you must pay or you get cut off is easy if you maintain it. I did not ask any questions in this section. Bills need to be paid. Period.

- If you can have an automatic bill paying online, then do it. The only problem with ACH (Automated Clearing House) is ensuring that you have the funds in the account when the bills need to be paid.
- The money that comes in needs to be allocated as soon as it hits the cash register. Think of each dollar as having a home and you need to put it there. Pulling funds out of the register for "petty cash" is the kiss of death. Your employees see you do it and figure they can too.
- Pay your bills first and fast. If you do get behind on paying bills, you will have a good track record with your vendors and be able to talk with them to get you through a rough patch.
- Have a place to place all invoices and bills. If you have one spot to be able to review your bills, you will be more likely to avoid missing paying one.
- The whole "Pay yourself first" stuff is for the money left over AFTER you pay your bills. That includes paying your royalties and advertising fees to the franchisor. You signed the contract and they are not a bank to make loans to you.

- Review every bill for accuracy. Like you, vendors are human(ish). They can make mistakes and you will have a hard time going back to get money from them rather than tackling an overcharge when it happens.

Customers are your homework too.

How in the world can you consider customers "homework"? Of course, I am going to ask a question to give you the answer. It is a book. How else would you get an answer? When is a person a customer? The answer is: When they come back. Your homework is to create situations where your customers want to come back.

The first visit is just to check you out and see if they can be comfortable being one of your customers. They are NOT a customer yet. They are more like stalkers. They watch, listen, and keep a close eye on you. These people are taking mental notes. If they can see themselves as one of your customers, they will be back. They are looking for specific things and if you do not deliver, they will go somewhere else next time. The first visit is for seeing if you want them.

The second visit is to see if you are consistent. That whole stalker thing is true. They are still watching you and deciding if they want to be your customer. The second visit is the most important. The general public will give you a pass, some of the time, if they do not see the best performance on a first visit. Most people understand you are human and things go wrong from time to time. If you let them know the mistakes are not typical, you can get them back for another try. If you show them the same kind of craziness that you showed them the first time around, they are gone for good. The second visit is critical.

The third visit is when they love you or hate you. Customers want to find a place they can call "theirs". They want to feel like they own the place and will bring others to make a point of being known as a customer. They are your best marketing efforts and the spot where you should spend the most effort. Great marketing plans mean nothing if what the customers experience is rotten.

Homework #14:

- Start by being your own customer. If you cannot listen and watch everything like a customer does, then find someone who can be critical and honest with you.
- Spend time with the customers. This is a great way to hear what they have to tell you. Listen for clues as to what they are saying. When a customer says, "Everything's fine" or "I'm good", there is something that is not making their experience outstanding. Outstanding experiences trump great marketing every time.
- Ask questions. When you get answers from customers, ask more questions. Typically, you should ask at least three questions and up to five questions. Do not ask more than five questions at any one time. Customers are there to be served, not to be grilled like their dinner.
- If you are not there, make it obscenely easy for customers to give you feedback. How many places can you give a customer the chance to give feedback? It is unlimited. How many places actually do this? Almost none. Be better than your competition. Let customers know you want to hear from them.
- Once you get feedback, follow up fast, fast, and fast. Customers who give feedback want to hear from you. Most of the time, they do not hear anything from a company. Pick up the phone and

call them; you will make them a fan for life. That is, if you do this every time they give you feedback. The cost of hiring an outside company to be a secret shopper and give you feedback costs a lot more then answering a real customer who wants to talk.

- Do great things for customers who keep coming back. Recognize customers, treat them to something special, and give them discounts. They can either stay your customer or leave and spend their money with the newest business in town. Discounts to existing customers sounds like taking money out of your pocket, but it is an investment in keeping them paying you. Just think what it would cost you to get that customer back in advertising and discounts. Compare the costs. Now you get it!

Homework takes time and effort and some money. You either pay the cost or you fail. It does not matter whether it is in high school or in business. Homework is the cost of getting a passing grade and staying in the game. Neglect it and you will start to spiral out of control. Remember the kids who did not graduate? Of course you do not. They are forgettable because they forgot to do the work alongside you. Do not be forgettable.

Lesson 15

There Are Grades??? What the...

There are grades...in franchising? Yes. There are grades in every business. There are websites designed to post feedback on how well you treat customers. If you think you are going to be great because of location, location, location as the Real Estate Department told you when you signed your agreement, you are wrong, well, almost wrong. A good location can make your business successful. It just won't keep it that way. The stores that graded well with customers are still around after the last economic dip. The rest are cold, dark shells.

Grades take many forms. The operations department in your franchise is going to give you a grade on your operations. The Health Inspector and the Building Code Authority will give you a grade too. The customers, the vendors, your bank, and anyone else you deal with will grade you and treat you according to that grade. If things are failing, you can get shut down.

Grades never go away. I bet you got a grade when you worked for a big corporation before jumping into franchising. Someone somewhere is grading everything you do. Just ask your kids how you are doing as a parent. They are going give you a grade too! OK, maybe we do not want to ask our kids how we are doing. They are easily swayed by a bowl of ice cream and a promise of sprinkles on top.

Grades are a way of letting you know if you are moving down the right path. It is a "map" of where you are and where you need to be. The smart kid franchisees are going to want to compare their grade with yours. The jocks and the nerds are going to want to know if they are better than you too. It is their way of feeling superior to you and everyone else in the franchise.

Comparing grades means nothing to you as a franchisee. It should be looked at on a store by store basis and no bigger than that. Let me repeat that last thought. Your grades or at least the grades for a particular location only go as far as the property line. Each business has its own culture and problems. Trying to compare one franchisee to another is a useless exercise. There are far too many variables to make a good comparison. Do not get me wrong. I want you to compare yourself to others. It is how we know where we stand. It is just not an indicator of how your business is doing. I can point to many million-dollar businesses that are failing. I can point to a small store with 500 square feet of business space that will let the owners retire when they want because it is incredibly profitable. Do not be fooled by averages and percentages. The story of your store is all that matters.

Just as a reminder, teachers in high school get graded too. If all their students fail, they will not be asked to come back the next year. That is why someone is going to pass her class. She wants to keep her job. She gets summers off for goodness' sake. She is going to teach to make the class look like they learned something and then work as a lifeguard all summer long. Take an average class and you will see that most kids land in the middle. Averages keep teachers in jobs and students moving along the conveyor belt of promotion through freshman to senior. Look at true growth per student (something that you will not see in most schools) and you find a whole new image. Taken individually, students can get great results when they review where they stand from one week to another. No, not month to month. The smaller the time frame for learning the better the results will be. Focus on one thing, sales, service, or item and you can make it work better. Look at averages and you will see nothing.

As a consultant, I want to show improvement in your franchise grades. If I am too lenient, someone will bust me for letting things slide and I will lose my job. Also, the store will get complaints from customers who love to bust us. I won't let things slide. There is a system and I will see what I see (yes, each part of your business) and mark it down. I am not going to "give" a grade when I inspect a store. I am going to call what I see and be surprised with the grade. If I look to "make" a grade, I am not doing anyone any good. Great operations happen when all things are done well.

In a franchise, grades are taken on these items:

- Cleanliness – If it is inside or outside the store and has anything to do with the store or the brand, keep it clean and organized. The health department, your franchisor and your customers are all going to grade you on how well you maintain your store. If you do not have a checklist full of cleaning duties with someone responsible for each job, then you are going to get a failing grade. Failing grades in cleanliness can shut you down for good.
- Fully Staffed – Having a fully staffed operation is important for many reasons, not just to keep things going. Yes, you need the right number of people doing the right number of things at the right time but, you also need to make it clear that understaffed teams mean that someone on the team is working extra hard to keep things going and will burn out and quit. Your customers will grade you on how well you staff your store to be ready to help them.
- Training – Having a team that is following the franchise system is critical. I went into a well-known burger franchise recently and left without food. It took too long at the register for the employee to ring up a burger, fries and a medium drink. I peeked over the register and saw that there are pictures of the products over the keys. PICTURES! The franchise gave up on training and changed their operations to meet a poorer quality

of employee. (Can you guess the franchise?) That just created an even lower quality of hiring pool that gave me, as the customer, nothing but grief. It is not the employee's fault. It is the owner's fault. It is the franchisor's fault. Train and keep training if you want better employees and loyal customers. Customers will grade you on how well you train yourself and your staff.

- Marketing Plans – If you are not following a marketing plan, you are failing. I have listened to every excuse on why franchisees do not like to advertise. If you think it takes money out of your pocket to give a discount or you have enough customers, sell and get out. It takes money out of your pocket to not advertise and give a discount. A smart coupon directed at customers makes a huge impact and can give you record profits. Marketing, as a definition, is inviting. If you are not inviting customers back with a coupon, an offer, or introducing a new product, then they are going to go somewhere else. All people follow paths. You go to work, you go home, you go to church, and you go your kid's school. Going to your store is way down on their list of things to do. If you do not have a marketing plan that invites customers in, you are failing, and I am going to grade you that way. Your customers are grading how well you invite them in.

- Products and Services – If you do not have a good, quality product and service, you are going to get a failing grade. Competition should keep you pursuing greatness. I have seen a few business owners over the years try to ignore this grade and hope that customers and the franchisor do not notice. If you spend any time at all in a business that provides exceptional service you won't forget it and you will compare every other business to that new standard of greatness. Customers grade you on products and service. They give you a failing grade by not coming back.
- Profitability – If you are pulling in great money, but not keeping any of it, then you are failing. I do not want anyone to fail, so I am going to ask for Profit and Loss Statements often. I want to see that you aren't running everything you can find through your business in order to show low/no profits. The government is still going to get the taxes owed. Trying to find ways to funnel profits away from your bottom line only makes the next crisis the last day your business will be open. Ever scratch your head and wonder why a restaurant that was packed would close for good suddenly? Something happened and they could no longer float the cost. Profits are what show a business's health.

Grades are needed and should be searched out. If you do not know how you are doing, ask. If you do not like the answer, do NOT kill the messenger or discount what you hear. Make changes if it matches your business plan and Franchise Agreement. Once you reach an A+ grade, you will not want to drop below that. At least, you should not. If you can get all "A's" then why settle for less.

There are far too many franchisees that get comfortable with mediocrity. They have RMS (Repetitive Motion Sickness) and cannot find a cure. They have been doing the same job for years operating a franchise and they do not want to change. The problem is in the fact that they changed and never noticed. I bet they are not operating their business the same way they did years prior. They just found the path of least resistance and stuck with that new path. The sad truth is that if they saw the service they provide when they are a customer, they would call for the manager's head and a full refund. RMS is a malady that requires drastic changes to get well again and most of the time it requires a new owner to fire the old staff. Training someone who is resistant to change is not worth the effort or cost.

Grades are needed and should be posted for your entire team to see and be graded by.

Lesson 16

There's Another Year of This?? REALLY!?!

Are you sure there is enough caffeine or booze to go another year in this nuthouse? Yes, there is. Get ready, catch your breath and start looking for something sturdy to hold on to. Your sophomore year is easier. You already know what not to do. By the way, what not to do is what franchisors and high school teachers do not spend enough time explaining. They figure that you will just follow along the plan that they created and not look outside the lines.

The old way of thinking that you will just sit still and take what they are dishing out to you is why there are so many people covered up with animosity, angst, stress and zits. Of course, I have never heard of a franchise CEO having his house rolled in toilet paper by franchisees, but that may happen if they do not change and listen to franchisees.

Another year in franchising makes you a sophomore. You have more knowledge than someone new but you still have that "new guy smell". Think about when you were in high school. Did being a sophomore give you special privileges or make life easier? If you think it did, you were just imagining it. Life after year one is just another year to get tripped in the hallway. The important thing that changes is that you know a little more about what to expect. Getting your mind around the need to work hard is the first step to making your life easier.

Being a sophomore feels like you have the right to start making comments on what should change for newbie's and how to get things done faster, easier, or at a cheaper cost. The problem is the same as when you were in high school...you are not in charge. You signed an agreement that you would follow the system and that they can change that system any way they want to. Does it seem like the cards are stacked against you? Of course they are. Did your high school teachers listen to you more when you became a sophomore? You were only thinking about freedom when you looked into buying a franchise and now you have crazy thoughts (yes, they are super crazy thoughts) that you can make a franchisor listen to reason. The short answer is that you have little credibility but not enough to change the direction of the company. The longer answer is that you can get them to follow you if you make a few strategic moves.

Credibility is something earned and, in franchising, years in business give you an edge. No executive is going to listen to a new franchisee as long as you are still seen as new. "New" in franchising means that you have not survived the storm yet. If they cannot see that you have the backbone to put up with crap from customers, vendors, and anyone in the franchise, then you have no credibility. There is a shortcut to getting credibility and it looks like a pile of money. Money makes people listen. No one has to like you, but people will listen if you can show that you can make money. Some of the worst personalities on the planet have the most credibility because they show they can make money. Is it wrong? Yes, but money talks. In high school, it was not the smartest kid who got the most attention; it was the kid with the most stuff. Stuff costs money so, money talks and builds credibility. Even the companies that give back to society post their earning as a benchmark to their credibility. Is it fair? No, but that's because money does not care who owns it and its value doesn't change because of who holds it.

As for me, the paragraph above makes me sad. It took me all of twenty years to get the credibility I have in franchise operations. This is mostly because they do not pay us well. Guys like me cannot buy respect (remember, they do not pay us well). We earn credibility every day and can lose it in seconds. Being a franchise consultant is the toughest job out there. We are graded on how other people and businesses perform. If a franchisee fails, we often lose our jobs. If someone gets hurt in a store, even if we were not there or had anything to do with it, we can lose our jobs. If there is an angry franchisee who yells at an executive in the franchise, we can lose our job. I do not hear of many high school teachers who lose their jobs if one student fails, has a meltdown, or gets hurt. Be kind - hug your franchise consultant. So how do you survive in a franchise? Do like your franchise consultant and find a good strategy.

Since money talks, how does a sophomore earn more profits and become credible? There are simple steps to becoming the most profitable franchisee in the chain. The first is the one that will shock and surprise you...follow the system you bought.

I am not a linear thinker. I do not like to follow the rails and just let things go where they are destined to go. I cannot leave things alone. I want to tinker. Does this sound like you? Most entrepreneurs have this way of thinking. We can fail in business when we think too far out of the box. I told you earlier that it took me twenty years to earn credibility. It took me twenty years to realize when to follow the system and when to break out and take it to the next level. That is the strategy that you need to learn as well.

Step one is and will always be follow the system. The thing about following the system that should be reassuring is that you do not have to create it from scratch. Think of it as being ten steps ahead of the guy trying to do it all on his own. You found a better way and that way was in a franchise. In high school, all you had to do was what they asked you to do. Once you got that settled, you had plenty of room to make a mess of things. The same is true now. Just remember to follow the path they plotted for you.

Step two is to look at how you are earning your money. The system works because it is a system. That does not mean that the system works for all your potential customers. Learn where your money comes from, and you can start to take the system to the next level. In every franchise, there is a new source of income. It can be products, services, or new groups to invite in to see what you do. Find out where your money is coming from can be a formal or an informal survey. It can be tracking customers by getting their home and email address. When you know who your customers are, look for the outliers. That is your new source of income. That is how to work within the system and still break the mold.

Step three is to bring the data to the franchisor and ask for feedback. Does that sound like you are giving away the recipe for the secret sauce? By getting the franchisor involved, you have a new partner in grabbing even more customers with their use of branding and marketing dollars spent. Bring them the data and you will see that they can help you grow faster than if you worked by yourself.

Step four is brag about it. How in the world are you going to make a franchise change direction if they do not know they need to listen to you? How did the kid who just got a new pair of sneakers let you know to look at his feet? He bragged about it. Show them, tell them, and make a big old fuss about finding a new way to make more money.

There you go! You now have a plan to be a badass and not get kicked out. It works in high school and in franchising. Just be aware of the fact that there are other sophomores and they are going to do the same thing as you. Use your strategy for the good of the brand and you win. Try to make a change to the system that you liked when you bought it and you will be in detention or get expelled. Franchising does not move without a reason. Do not waste the effort trying to move things without a pile of money to entice it to move your way.

The Prom King Can't Dance

Your high school prom is the exact same fiasco as the annual convention in a franchise. Everyone dresses well and smells nice. Pictures are taken and everyone tries to be on their best behavior (at least until some brings out the booze). There are smiles, hugs, and good feelings all around. There is excitement in the air and the possibilities of what the night could bring are endless.

It is a time when everyone gets together in a fancy hotel ballroom and eats expensive "institutional" food (it's the equivalent of the school lunch on nicer plates and its usually chicken). Cliques come together for cover as everyone gets eyeballed for the clothes they are wearing. Stories are told around the tables about what happened in the last year and then the ceremony begins.

Both events have got to be the strangest coming of age ceremonies that ever existed. If you are in a franchise and think you already came of age, think about how excited you are to find out who the franchisee of the year is and who gets recognized on stage. Each and every year you get to relive the "moment" when you get all dressed up for the fun of it and every year you wonder why you spent the time and money to hang out with people you didn't even like. It's because you think you are going to change in some small way if you come the convention and it will bring you to the next level of whatever it is you are thinking a franchisee can be. This is the lie we create around the ceremony. It is enormous fun to watch.

At prom time, we do change. It is a coming-of-age ceremony when you put aside your childish ways and start thinking about becoming an adult. Prom is the line in the sand when you get to party because you are losing your youth and moving on to the next stage in your life. It is all ceremonial, but it works. Kids start thinking about college and work and families and responsibilities. Man, if we could go back and tell our younger selves just what life is really all about. But we cannot. Life moves on.

By the way, no, the Prom King can't dance just like the Franchisee of the Year can't dance. Neither of them was elected to be able to show off some sweet dance moves. The "king" was elected because he was the most likeable guy in the voting class. That should speak volumes about what other people are trying to tell you to think about the school or the brand. He is the person that a school or franchise holds up as the "best of the lot". It is the story you need to pay close attention to whether you are a freshman or if you have been a franchisee forever. It is the story of the brand and the statement of what is important to it and who is in charge of shining a light on the image they want you to see.

For my readers who think I am way off base by correlating the high school prom king with the franchisee of the year, let me break it down for you.

- The Prom King is elected by the senior class (with the Administration having the right to veto someone they do not like, agree with, or is failing).
- The Franchisee of the Year is voted on by the Executive Team and maybe some of the underlings like me in the operations department (with the Executive team having the right to veto someone they do not like, agree with, or is failing).
- He/she is the most likeable person in the class.
- He/she is probably the most tolerable (yes, I do mean to write tolerable) person with the highest sales in a franchise. The guy who brings in the most money isn't a shoo-in for the Franchisee of the Year. They just need for him to be OK with winning and not too big dork about it.
- Neither the prom king nor the franchisee of the year is elected because they can dance even though there is usually dancing after he is "crowned". The idea is that they are moving the way the brand wants them to.

Why do we have a convention if we are already adults with all the responsibility we can handle? In very simple terms, it is to redirect you to a new way to move your business because the FDD contract wasn't enough to motivate you to follow the requirements every time. There are no two franchisees that are alike just like there are not two high school students that are the same, but that doesn't mean that the administration isn't going to stop trying to get everyone to dance to their music.

Prom and convention are a way of getting the groups to move to something nicer than what they see every day. Wearing a tux or an evening gown is not something that most people put on in the morning unless you are an actual king or some kind of debutante. Why do it then? Why go to the trouble of dressing up? It changes your perspective. How that works, my friends, is the key to changing a person's vision and is the reason there is a prom, a convention, and a prom king or franchisee of the year.

If you want to change a person, you change the way other people look at him. No, you do not start with how the person sees himself. You start by changing how and why others see them.

My apologies go to any psychotherapists reading this paragraph. I know you think you have to dig out some childhood memory to get to the root of whom you are, but that is hogwash. It is not going to work to try to make someone act differently if you show them who they are. Try to tell someone to calm down and show them how to take a deep breath. Does that work? Of course it doesn't work. You didn't change their environment. You literally added to their anxiety. Change the situation and people will change the way they react. Now, calm down and keep reading slowly. If you are a psychotherapist reading this book, call me. I have unresolved issues. Nah, forget it. I'm too old to change and I think my issues make me endearing.

Dressing a certain way is a clear example of changing an environment. Dress nicely and people will react to you nicely. Dress sloppily and you will be treated as sloppy. Why does this work? It is because everyone is inherently lazy, lazy, and lazy.

You have so many things swirling around in your head at any one time that deciding on how to treat the person in front of you drops into a predetermined bucket. You do not have time to really get to know someone new, so you take a quick look and make a decision. After that, you mostly stick to that decision. It is only after repeated interactions or a shocking transformation that you will change our mind. So, we get all dressed up to try to get a new image of the person in your class or your brand. After all, who has the time and energy to keep looking at someone with the hope that he will change. Convention is sometimes the first or only time in a year that you will be in the same room with people who are helping or hurting your business. Seeing them in a new, better way can change the way you treat them for the next 365 days. Hence, we have conventions, proms, and events.

The Prom King or Franchisee of the Year is the top of the food chain when it comes to the perception of the brand or the school. Popularity aside, you have to be something that the school or brand wants to show off. Ever seen an ugly prom king? Likewise, have you ever seen a franchisee with an ugly store that wins the top spot? Homely wins some of the time, but ugly is a strict no-win. There is an image that the school or brand wants you to aim for for the rest of the year. And they parade it in front of you on stage.

> Disclaimer: If you went to a school where the weird kid won Prom King, there was probably some kind of joke going on around the school and you should be ashamed of yourself. If you had a franchisee of the year who was not someone you would have ever thought could win, there is something of a joke going on and you should sell and get out. Remember what I said at the beginning of this chapter? This is the way for the brand to show you what they want you to be. If they elect to have the guy who is causing problems as franchisee of the year, then you should be scared. There is a breakdown in the vision of the brand. It is one of the reddest red flags to see.

If you are in a franchise that has more than one top franchisee, then you are a source of income for the franchisor. Is this a problem? You should know that you are expendable. The executive team is making decisions without a care to who you are or what you do as long as they get the royalty checks when they are due. I have worked with many franchises that think they can have a dozen or more franchisees of the year. You do not have to sell your business to be safe. You do have to look, as they do, at your business as a source of income. With any income, you should not have all your money coming from one source. I can almost guarantee that there is more than one brand in the franchise and they are in constant growth mode by adding new franchisees every year.

For my franchisor friends, this book is meant to shine a light on the happenings in a franchise. I do not disagree with you that making money is a good thing. I just want you do be honest. If you are honest, then your franchisees will be honest and everyone can move on to griping about something more important. You may think that you are being sneaky or that you can do as you want, but there is more to people than being a royalty for you. The best franchises are honest, open, and caring when it comes to their franchisees. Those franchises are usually family owned and have a few family members as franchisees. That is how you build a legacy brand. More on that is for another book from me.

If you think you want to skip the prom (i.e., the convention), make sure you are legally able to skip it. Deep inside the FDD is a line or two on training requirements. If it states that you must be at convention, then you have got to go. Dust off your dancing shoes and have fun. After all, you have the chance to take advantage of the time away from your business to unwind. Do not unwind too far though. There is a reason the franchisor wants to see you. The Principal can make your life easier if you show up and behave. At least, he won't make life tougher on you out of spite. So, once your time watching the show and shaking hands ends, run off to do what you want. You are your own business owner within the brand. Enjoy it!

Lesson 18

There Is No Summer Break in Franchising

Do you want to know another reason people fail in a franchise? They think like high school kids when it comes to time off. In high school, you could count on time off. It was scheduled and you were prepared to be free of responsibility and homework. The only people more interested in getting some time off than you were the teachers. You knew you had weekends, Spring break, and summer vacation. Not once did you think you may have to go to school for an emergency. There was not a time when you knew you had to cover a class for another student because he called in or quit. Life in high school was clear and uncluttered.

Fast forward to you-as-a-franchisee and things are a lot different. You are the owner. You are in charge and need to be on call any time of the day in order to make sure the investment you made in your business doesn't fail. There are no real breaks in franchising. Even when you are away from the franchise, you are still thinking about the business. Since your first day as a franchisee, you have not had a conversation when you were not thinking about some part of work. And, just so you know, everyone around you can see it in your eyes when you are talking with them. Life as a franchise owner is all responsibility on you.

For those franchisees reading this who think I am being dramatic, I will refer you to the last paragraph and let you think about what was going through your head when you read it. I bet at least twice you thought of something that you need to do or to direct someone else to do in your store. Over a couple decades, I have found that the people who think they can just walk away from their franchise and play are the first ones crying about not having great sales or customer counts. They are the ones who are being robbed by all of the "trustworthy" employees hired so they can have summer off. There is no free time in franchising. That is, unless you create it.

How do you deal with always being "Atlas" holding the world on his shoulders? The quick answer is that you just do it. Being in charge was what you bought when you handed a check over to the sales weasel. The longer answer is how you deal with being out of control. It is something you mastered as in high school if you were not that creepy nervous kid that chewed on his notebooks, pencils, and the occasional desk. Being out of control and being ok with it is the way to find balance in franchising and is something that takes years to master. Freshmen are going to suffer. I have a hug for you if you need one.

The first thing you need to know is that owning a franchise location is a numbers game. If you want a day off, you need to set the stage for that to happen. Break the game into semesters. You remember how this works from high school, don't you? Focus on the first semester first. If you think you can tackle the entire year on day one, you are OCD and need mental help. Franchising, and most of life, is all about pacing.

Remember the dance from the last chapter? Find the groove and you will set the pace for the entire business. In order to have time off, you have to work for it. When you set the pace for the marathon that is your new career as a franchisee from the first day, you will be better prepared to handle the chaos. And there is plenty of chaos every day. If you ever have a day when there is not something going wrong, then you are missing something. I will help you learn how to be OK with that if you listen and learn. It is how you can grow and learn to be less upset with the things that go wrong because life is messy and business ownership is a junk yard of steaming piles of, well, you know.

Let's start with the basics. A good rule of franchising is that numbers rule. If you know how much you need to pay the bills (i.e., the break-even point) then you will know what you need to bring in each day to survive. Counting the costs of surviving another day, week, and month is the first test of any good business. In high school, you figured out the first week what was required for you to pass the class. It is the same way in business. When you were in high school, did you think about the grade you wanted to end the semester with on the first day of class? How much better would you have done in school if you had and aimed for an "A"? Aren't you smarter now than you were in high school?

Take all the bills that you have for the month and get a total. Are these set amounts or do they fluctuate? Will your food costs go up around holidays? Will your labor costs go up in the summer? Give it a good estimate and figure it out for the year. Break that number down into weeks (there are 52 of them each year). That is what you need to bring in each week to survive the year. Minimums count when you are in business. If you cannot hit the minimums, then you need to change the cost of doing business. Survival is necessary. Remember all the statistics on how many businesses fail in the first year? It is because they have the wrong break-even point for the money they bring in.

You can hire me to go over how to increase your sales, lower your costs or change your business model to get your sales in line with the amount of money needed. I am not inexpensive to hire. Add that into your break-even number.

Survival plus well used profits equal success

Once you add into the equation the need to grow, you are getting closer to having one day off. Add in the amount needed to add another location and you are looking at the first "A" of the first semester. Do I mean for you to give that crazy franchisor more hard-earned money for another Franchise Agreement? Yes. Hang on! It gets even better!

Franchising and small business is all a numbers game. To have the life the sales weasel so eloquently talked about when you first met him, you have to spend more than you originally thought. One store means a lot of risk. If that location fails, you fail. Having more than one location gives you balance in your earnings. Your financial advisor has been telling you forever that you should diversify. Having more than one location means you have more than one place to earn a living. The road in front of one of your stores can be shut down because the Department of Transportation decides they want to repave the road and you will still survive.

More than one location means that you can share employees between stores, you can buy in bulk and save on costs, you can even get better prices when you bundle costs of phones, internet, and insurance. Using multiple stores to even out your portfolio is smart. It also means that the chaos of business gets a little more controlled. You have more people to help keep things working and a "pipeline" of employees to train up to manage the chaos. Does that make you feel better?

Now that you can (hopefully) total all the amount of money needed daily to run your business and the amount needed to add another franchise to your portfolio, you must go earn it. I will make an assumption that you have the money to be in business for longer than a month. That is Bulldog Rule for Business #2. (Visit BusinessBulldog.com) That should move up to the number one position. Read them all and see what you think. If no one asked you if you have the resources to stay in business longer than a month before you signed the FDD and you handed them the franchise fee, then you have other problems.

Let's be really, really clear here. You are not going to buy the big house or the expensive anything when you have profits from one or a few stores. You will take only as much money out of your business what you need to have your family survive. The rest goes into covering slow weeks and adding to the bank account to buy another store. I watch owners on a daily basis fail because they want things before they can afford them. Please do not be one of them.

Earning enough is not the point of this chapter. Earning enough to have a day off and having the structure to keep your business going with the best possible operations is the only thing that matters. By the way, there is never enough money. No, I am not being greedy. It is all about the need to plan for the worst and expect the best. I would give credit to whoever came up with that gem of a concept if I could find out who the author is. All good businesses have a foundation of planning for a crisis and expecting that nothing bad will happen because you already planned for the worst possible thing to happen. The entire insurance industry is based on that idea, and they seem to be doing pretty good.

Lesson 19

There's a Whole New Freshman Class Coming In

Did you think you were one of the last ones who was going to buy into the franchise? Do not be a silly franchisee. The franchisor of whatever concept you bought into is going to pack the house. They are going to add as many franchisees as they can without putting them on the same side of the street (and sometimes they'll do that too). It is their job. If you are successful, they will try to add more stores to capture even more of the market share. If you are not successful, they will add more stores to capture more of the market share. See any logic in it? Of course not! Logic isn't the reason for adding new franchisees. Adding franchisees is all about bringing in new blood to energize the brand and give customers someplace new to spend money. Oh yes, the biggest reason is to add more revenue to the franchisor's bottom line. Why did you get into business? It is the same reason.

More means more to a franchisor. Forget the fact that you built the market and that without you risking everything there would not be a market for them to try to shoehorn more franchisees into with less risk for them and less rewards for you. Franchising ain't fair. Get over it and make it all about you and your business. Brand your stores under the franchise brand name. Win by winning the war on best-in-class. I will pass the same brand to get to the one store I know I like. So will a lot of other customers and they will bring friends too. Stop wasting time and energy on trying to reason with them and crush the freshmen with experience.

The freshman class is going to come in like a dog coming out of the rain. They are going to rush in, shake things around, and smile while wondering why they are not getting more attention. All the while, you are looking at the mess they made and the mess that they are presenting to you and the world.

This new group of shiny-faced freshmen will be running into the room, your store, asking you a million questions and wondering how you stay in business or giving you grief about some part of your business that needs work. They will be as stubborn as you were and will drive you nuts. New franchisees, like high school freshmen, have no idea what they are doing but are ready to jump in feet-first hoping that someone will save them from themselves. For Franchise Consultants like me, we watch them with equal parts amusement and fear when they slam open the front doors as freshmen will do when they come into a franchise. All Franchise Consultants want the best for them since we are graded on how well they do. We also know they are like a three-year-old before Christmas. We love the energy these freshmen have since they haven't gotten worn down by the system yet. We also know that when the crash happens, and it will, we will be blamed for everything going upside down. Does that sound wrong? Of course, it does now that you have outlived your own stupidity. Speaking of your own stupidity, I want to take a minute for you to reminisce on the "good old days".

- Remember when you first tried to advertise or hire an employee? CRINGE!
- Remember when you thought you knew how to run the business only to find out just how little you did know? CRINGE!
- Remember when you thought opening the doors was a sure sign for customers to stroll in and spend buckets of money? CRINGE!
- Remember the thought of being your own boss and having time to go relax? OK, that one does not make me cringe. I do, however, shrug my shoulders and let that one go. I see far too many people with delusions of grandeur who think just being a business owner will somehow make their life better that I cannot even put the effort into cringing.

Freshmen are a tiring, trying group of blind mice running around a room. They love to tell you stuff. I know more about some people than their own spouses know. I am not a better person for having this information and in one case, I feel downright dirty hearing the evening activities of one of my former franchisees. I washed my ears out a dozen times after getting off of that phone call. Ugh! Do not misunderstand the situation when I say I know a lot about the franchisees. I need to know what makes you tick. There are a million reasons to be in business. There are equally as many motivators to get out and start something new. I need to know why you want to subject yourself to franchising. You are in business with all the fun people you thought you left in high school and now, you have the freshmen class stomping through your store wondering why you haven't failed. Life repeats itself.

Life repeats itself.

That smug feeling of superiority you have when you see the new franchisees come in the room is going to be a sick feeling in your stomach when you see that they have a good first month in business. Why in the world would they step into a business and do well when you struggled to turn a profit? It is because you already did the struggling for them. Customers already know the brand because you brought it to their attention. They love what you do so, they are going to love the newest store. It is, after all, a sparkling new store. And, it has to be just as good as what you do since it has the same name above the door as yours. Now, how is that sick feeling in your stomach? Breathe slowly into the paper bag and lean against something soft. The feeling will pass soon.

Watching an existing franchisee deal with a new franchisee is like watching a big dog deal with a Chihuahua on Red Bull. There is a lot of movement and not a lot of help. Stepping back and letting things slow down is the best answer to the question of what the big dog should do. New franchisees, like cheerleaders, get tired and find a new way to make things work. As the guy in the middle of all the action, I like to think about standing in the middle of a hurricane. Not that I have ever been in the eye of an actual hurricane, but I can imagine seeing the storms swirling around me everywhere I look. Yes, it is nice and calm where I stand, but I am still surrounded by the flying debris and can very easily get pulled into it. I am at my best when I walk along inside the storm and let things die out. There is usually a VP of something who wants to know why I have not squashed the storm. I would like to see a VP squash a melee like a new franchisee and an existing franchisee butting heads. I say let them! Once they are tired, I get to work making them get along.

As a new freshman, you have energy and enthusiasm. You have a whole movie of what it is going to be like being a franchise business owner playing in your head. And it is an award-worthy movie. I love to hear you talk about how great life will be and how you will have everything you want. I used to get all caught up in the soundtrack and sign along with new owners. It is a catchy tune and one that can brighten your day. One of the best freshmen I remember used to say, "I'm living the dream". That is nice. Of course, after he got past the initial grace period when customers got tired of the new store and went back to the most convenient store, he was saying something I do not want to write. There are too many bad words that would place this book in a bad part of the library. Freshmen are rollercoasters that have a huge highs and dazzling dips that will make you see your heart jump out of your chest. Being near them is just as crazy.

I Can Do This as Many Times as I Want

You may be asking why so many people jump into a new franchise even if they have been freshmen before this. I believe it is like being a parent for the second and third time. You forget how insane it is and only remember the good stuff. After all, you survived right? So, they jump into a franchise they have no business being in because they feel they can survive anything. Those reality stars that go out into the jungle naked to survive for three weeks would not make it in franchising. You can weave a suit out of banana leaves but finding a way to cover payroll when you are floating payments and trying to keep your marriage together while living in your store is a whole other reality. Go ahead; try sleeping while you have people asking for money every day. I know what tough looks like. I have lived it from the corporate side of franchising and held people together while they let time and good business practices bring them out of the hole. Why someone would be a freshman again and again is a mystery to me.

God love the existing franchisees who think they are being beaten out of sales because they are successful and now have a new competitor in their own brand. It is really sweet how they think they can have the entire pie and eat it too. Bless their stupid hearts. They forgot to read their Franchise Agreement for how close the franchisor can put another store, or they did not think it applied to them. You just want to hug them till they stop making stupid statements about being run out of business.

I can tell you how many times it has happened where a franchisor put a franchisee out of business when they added a store to the market. I remember two times. One time the franchisee spent so much time spying on the new store that his staff stole everything out from under his nose and the other time was when the franchisee was so mad that we would add another store to "his" town that he just closed his store. I do not know what personality that is in high school. I do not remember anyone quitting high school because freshmen came in but, I may have missed it.

If you feel that I'm little tough on existing franchisees when they whine about new franchisees coming into the system, I am. The idea is that you can work with them and make your franchise brand own the town and push out all competitors or you can battle each other. Do not make the mistake of thinking I want all the same franchise stores on the same street. There is a right way to bring in the freshmen and there is a really bad way to do it.

The effective way to bring in freshmen is to let the existing franchisees know there is going to be a new franchisee in the market and introduce them. Scratch that. Start at the beginning. Let the existing franchisees know you have a space to fill in a market and then see who wants to add another store. That way, everyone is in on the growth strategy. No one is missing the chance to grow near their current store. If a new franchisee comes in, then there is no whining allowed.

The bad way of bringing in a freshman is to just spring it on everyone. The new store just pops up like a mushroom in your yard. (Have you ever noticed that mushrooms are just there? One day there is no mushroom. The next day, boom, a field of mushrooms shows up). Get tunnel vision in your business and there are a lot of things that happen without being noticed. Do not let that happen. Ask your consultant if there is a possibility of another franchisee coming into your market soon. The fact that you are asking can be the catalyst for keeping the market yours for a while longer. It can also get people asking questions about how many stores they can add. Ask anyway.

Make freshmen your own personal minions!

Who does not like minions? I mean they are happy to help since you are there to coach them on what needs to be done, right? I like the idea of minions as long as it is a two-way street. The minion approach is good since it requires that you mentor the new franchisee. In addition, there are a lot of good things that you get from being the coach:

- You can have them put in money from their marketing fund to help advertise their store and yours. Cutting marketing costs can save big bucks.
- You can share employees when things get busy.
- You can create your own buying co-op to buy supplies in bulk and split the cost and savings.

- You can feed off their enthusiasm. Attitudes are contagious.

Find your best way of working with the new franchisees. They are going to come in and they are either going to help you make more money or they are going to fight you every step of the way. What story is written in the franchise history is up to you. I have seen franchisees go out of business trying to fight another franchisee in the same brand and I have seen them work so well together, you would think they were business partners in all of the stores.

What story will be told about you when the freshmen come trampling in?

Lesson 20

The Senior Class Project

This is a great place to let you know that karma is real and will bite you on the butt if you have a crappy attitude toward the freshman class. As a senior, being a mentor to the minions is an option as I wrote about in the last chapter. The opposite of being helpful will make you the most hated person in the brand. Now, being an "Evil Overlord" sounds like great fun and allows you to wear a cape and freak out people with an evil laugh, but it is the kiss of business death. Bad people get bad results.

Attitudes are contagious. When you are successful, you have a great attitude, and everyone wants to help make you more successful. A bad attitude is like a virus. It is even easier to pass along to other people than a good attitude. Want to experiment with this theory? Go to the grocery store. Watch a customer complain about something to a cashier. When the customer leaves, the problem is gone, right? Nope. The cashier will be angry for at least the next five customers. They need a good customer to bring them back to a state of happiness. It works the same on your wife when you are crabby ass. But happiness comes back when you buy jewelry, set it on the table carefully, step back quickly, and apologize profusely. Some experiments are not recommended and just flat-out dangerous. Do not be a crabby ass to your wife.

Being the south end of a north-bound mule toward new franchisees makes you the jerk. No, they are not being jerks by coming into your market. The franchisor is the one that sold the agreement to them. And they want to be near you to start with some of the magic you created. New businesses, more often than not, bring new customers. Everyone is interested in how things work in a new location. They can either be a great representation of the brand and in a direct line, you. Or, they can be horrible because you have been bullying them since you found out they were coming and that crappy attitude bled over to your customers who are checking them out and are now going to go to the competitor's brand because you both have rotten attitudes. To a customer all businesses with the same logo are the same. Have a bad experience in one place and all of the stores with the same name are seen as bad.

Bullying the new guy is a bad idea. You think you own the market and have done all the heavy lifting to get the success that you have and do not want a new guy arriving and destroying it. I get that way of thinking. Dealing with group dynamics is a tricky skill especially if you are in the group. If, however, you think about keeping that image and loyalty going, even with competition from someone under the same logo, you need to make sure the new guy has all the right information. Protecting your brand by helping the new guy sounds wrong but it is not. It is your senior project.

Why would the franchise bring someone in that you now have to spend time working with when they could just try to make you more successful? It is the same reason schools integrated, and we do not have all boy or all girl schools anymore. Franchises work best when all the franchisees bring their own culture to the business under one brand. When the first franchisees in the brand started, they thought they were successful. Then, they brought you in. You showed them a whole new level of success. So, doesn't it make sense to try to bring the brand to the next level? That means bringing in the next star students. You can either help them as they start in the franchise and ride the wave to the next level or you can be bitter and sell your business. It is your senior project. What is it going to look like when you finish?

I get the fact that all franchisees question the system they bought into. They should. You can bring this paragraph with you when you talk with the corporate hacks. If the corporate office thinks that the only good ideas come from them, sell and run. I have had Vice President's of Operations with a billion-dollar brand tell me that I was thinking too much and that all ideas came from him. What a dork! I got out of that brand quickly after that stupid message. As the franchisee, you should question things that come down the pipe. It is your livelihood. Now that you know why they bring in a whole new freshman class, you can be a part of the legacy of the brand.

Let's talk about the new guy. Dealing with him is tough. He wants to steal all your employees and will probably grab a few as they see something new as a way of bettering their work life. Let them go. You do not own them. Do not blame the new owner for hiring them. Wouldn't you hire someone who is already trained and ready to hit the ground running? Of course you would. Stop lying that you have integrity and would NEVER do that. I have seen pastors and the most honest people you can meet hire another store's employee right out from under the nose of the franchisee.

Have an agreement from the first meeting that the new guy will call you when one of your employees wants to work for him. No, it is not to give the employee a hard time (remember that bullies get bad things). If you give the employee a hard time, you are going to get sued. Also, you cannot talk about how they were as an employee. That is confidential. All you can say is whether you would hire the employee back. I am not acting as a lawyer or your personal HR department. There are rules that you cannot cross. Do not start talking about how an employee worked for you or you are going to get in hot, hot water.

Work with the new guy to save money. Buy in bulk and split the cost as much as you can. The savings all go to the bottom line. More money for you is what the name of the game is all about.

Be ready for them not to be prepared to handle the costs, workload, and stress. They are going to freak out at some point. It is all part of them growing up in business. High school showed you what that looks like. Freshmen came in freaked out and stayed that way for most of the year. Of course, as soon as they calmed down, they got a face-full of pimples and their voice changes. Can you imagine if by the second year in a franchise your voice changed? The pimples would make you cranky, but the voice change would crack me up! We can only imagine the fun.

Lesson 21

Graduate! You Sell Out!

It has been an unbelievable time and now you have got to go. It was good to know you, but all things come to an end. Thanks for playing. Is anyone going to tell you when it is time for you to sell and go from a franchise? Yes, yes, we will. The feeling is the same whether you are in high school or a business. Your life as you know it is about to get turned on its head. Good luck and best wishes. There is the door...do not let it hit you on the backside when you are leaving.

When you started in high school, the first thought you had on the first day of school was "When can I get out of here?" When you bought a franchise license, did you think the same thing? You should have. When you decide to buy into a franchise, you have to think about the day that you will no longer be able to operate it and will eventually sell it. Even if you want to pass it on to your kids, you have to be prepared to do that with as little hassle as possible. After all, you spent your kids' childhood telling them to clean up their room. Turning a business over to them when the books and the operations look like a tornado went through it is not the best way to get them to want to take it over.

That weird kid who had all of his pencils equally sharpened and lined up on his desk was on to something. No, not the

OCD crazy lining up his pencils, but he was ready for school to start. He was obsessed about being prepared to start the school day and already had applications to universities that he wanted to go to ready to be mailed. He was ready for the last day of school on the first day. What were you doing? The OCD kid was also the reason you left corporate life since he drove you nuts with his micromanagement but, hey, you go to be your own boss, right?

Start before the first day you open to track everything. It is the same as buying supplies for the first day of high school. Make a list of what you need and the cost to buy it. Tracking costs makes all the difference in business. When I say you should track costs, I mean everything you can think of tracking. If it is supplies to clean the store or a product that sits on the shelf, the more you know what something costs to own, the more you will know where your money is going. I do not like statistics since they can be manipulated to look good or bad. Averages are more important. What is the average time it takes before you sell a product? Selling your business with that kind of information adds value to the sale and gives you something more to sell than just the business.

Let's talk about your Permanent Record for a minute. Go ahead and make an icky face. Permanent Records are one of those things that most kids were hoping was a myth. We hoped it was a scare tactic that teachers used to keep us in line. It was real! Of course, we grew up when it was a paper copy and there is a real chance that it no longer exists. The high school kids now have a digital permanent record, it is in the cloud forever and no one can make it disappear, truly permanent record. Sorry kids.

As for you in business, you want to have a permanent record. It is the Balance Sheet. It tells you all you need to know about your business (if it is up to date and uses good recording methods). It is the health report for the business. It tracks over the years what it costs to be in business. If your accountant is not keeping the Balance Sheet up to date, fire him and find one who can. The more trends you can see in the Balance Sheet the better the value of the document and the better value your business is when you sell it to the next guy who thinks owning a business will change his life for the better.

Getting out is not as easy as tossing the keys to someone else. There is a lot to do to keep the value up. If you do a little work each month, you can sell the business for more than what you paid and walk away happily. Sounds like something your Momma said when you were in high school. Mommas are smart like that. A little work now makes a big difference later. Study now and you will become an expert in 10,000 hours, right? Well, you are not going to spend 10,000 hours all night before the big exam studying and you aren't going to get your business ready to sell in the days before the closing. Start getting ready to sell before you even start.

Now, get out of the franchise and be nice about it. There will be no toilet paper rolls thrown in the trees in front of the business on the night of the sale. There will not be any bad words said, or fingers pointed northward in salute. You will leave nicely and calmly. If you believe that happens, you are right. Most franchisees who sell go quickly to the door and do not look back. Now, the ones who decide to burn every bridge before they leave are the stuff of legend. The franchisee who leaves a "present" in the vent for the next owner to find after it 'ferments" for a few days is cliché. The guy who put out coupons for free products before the sale is more creative. The guy who pays for a bus to load up homeless people to get free cleaning services is legendary. Please do not be like any of these guys. Lawyers love to take their profits from the sale if the business when you do stupid things like that.

You bought the business to change your life and hopefully it was a change for the better. Selling your business should be just as good. Find a good buyer. Someone who buys your business should be as diligent as you were and keep the good brand name going. Selling for cash rewards is a sad sight. Everything that kept you up at night worrying about will be turned into reality in the weeks following your departure. Who do you think everyone will blame?

Your job is to keep things moving when you are gone. Yes, you will mentor the new owner into your position. No, it is not your job to do so, but when you think about what you built, did you see it falling apart? Of course you did not. Spend the time and effort to keep your employees employed and the business running. Be proud of what you accomplished and walk away with dignity. Be remembered fondly.

The end is always near. Years pass quickly. Remember how fast high school flew by? Be prepared to go to the next chapter in your life right now. Once you sell (or graduate) you will have the time to do what you want. What you do with that time is up to you. Make the time to start thinking about your next plans now.

Conclusion

Like Most of Us, Books Have Endings

Yes, all good things come to an end and so does my writing of your new favorite book. I hope you learned a few things and it made you think about people and the work you do differently. I love working with people and changing the angle with which they view their world. A couple of degree difference can make a whole pile of money and drive happiness to your front door.

If you want to ask me a question or need me to help with your business, please email me at Questions@BusinessBulldog.com.

The more you question, the more you learn. That is, only if you ask the right question and spend the effort to listen.

Bless your hearts & all that ruckus.

Bob Griffin
Chief Bulldog-in-Charge

Business Bulldog

1 – Have the right reason for getting into business

2 – Have the money to get into business and stay in business

3 – All businesses are a people businesses

4 – The right people never want to work with the wrong people

5 – Train and then keep training your employees

6 – Reward the right actions by your employees

7 – Plan for small wins daily

8 – Dream about where your business can go and then make it happen

9 – Re-examine your business often

10 – You may not be the right person for the job

11 – Leave the emotion out of your business (most of the time)

12 – Not every person who enters your store is a customer